COUNTING
EVERY
VOTE

Related Titles from Potomac Books

Presidents' Most Wanted: The Top 10 Book of Extraordinary Executives, Colorful Campaigns, and White House Oddities—Nick Ragone

Personality, Character, and Leadership in the White House: Psychologists Assess the Presidents—Steven J. Rubenzer and Thomas R. Faschingbauer

The Cure for Our Broken Political Process: How We Can Get Our Politicians to Resolve the Issues Tearing Our Country Apart—Sol Erdman and Lawrence Susskind

COUNTING EVERY

VOTE

The Most Contentious Elections in American History

Robert Dudley AND **Eric Shiraev**

POTOMAC BOOKS, INC.
WASHINGTON, D.C.

Library of Congress Cataloging-in-Publication Data
Dudley, Robert L.
  Counting every vote : the most contentious elections in American history / Robert
Dudley and Eric Shiraev. — 1st ed.
     p. cm.
  Includes bibliographical references and index.
  ISBN 978-1-59797-224-6 (alk. paper)
  1. Presidents—United States—Election—History. 2. Contested elections—United
States—History. 3. United States—Politics and government. I. Shiraev, Eric, 1960–
II. Title.
  JK524.D7783 2008
  324.973—dc22

                                        2008024354

Potomac Books, Inc.
22841 Quicksilver Drive
Dulles, Virginia 20166

First Edition

10 9 8 7 6 5 4 3 2 1

CONTENTS

INTRODUCTION

Do Presidents Matter?

As a parlor game, speculating on how the nation, even the world, would have differed if only someone else had been elected president can be entertaining. Moreover, with the advantage of hindsight it can generate endless examples of how history might have been different. Illustrations of the spectacular alternative scenarios that come to mind might be:

- If Al Gore were elected president in 2000, America would not have fought the war in Iraq.
- If Hubert Humphrey were elected president in 1968, America would have been out of Vietnam in two years.
- If Charles Hughes had defeated Woodrow Wilson in 1916, America would have joined the League of Nations and probably would have avoided the war with Japan twenty-five years later.

Of course, nothing is that simple if we avoid sheer speculation. For example, President Al Gore would have faced a confrontational Congress in 2001, which would have seriously limited his policy options. Under President Hubert Humphrey, the United States would have faced a hostile and unpredictable China, still inhospitable to the United States and reaching to restore its formerly friendly relations with Russia. Presi-

1

dent Charles Hughes, most probably, might have mishandled the war economy in 1917 by refusing to raise taxes and establish federal regulations to help American labor.

History judges achievement first. We conveniently say that history, and not our perceptions of it, is the final reviewer of each president and what he has contributed—or not—to America and the world. Moreover, we can also say that it is the general course of history—fate, as it were—and not necessarily the leader's individual personality that matters in global developments. For example, according to a well-accepted point of view, American presidents play only a limited role in history. This is due to the particular structure of the American political system. This arrangement generally prevents presidents from making decisions that are politically unpopular in the short run, even though those decisions have the potential to be significant over time.[1]

We disagree with this point of view. Over the course of American history, presidents have made many great and dreadful decisions because of who they were. Presidents embark on some courses of actions and disavow others because of their individual traits and the unique historical circumstances in which they have served. Accounts of the decision-making process regarding the League of Nations in 1919, the decisions made about Vietnam in the Lyndon Johnson White House, the Watergate affair in the Nixon administration, the Iran Contra scandal in the Reagan White House, the decisions on the war in Iraq in 2001–02, and many other history-making developments point to the vital importance of individual choices in a democratic state.

One does not have to subscribe to the "Great Man" theory of history—attributing everything to a great leader—to believe that it matters who the president is or that it matters what the president does. Every president brings something new to the institution of the presidency. Each president has been a leader whose behavior and policies have, for good or bad, transformed the country. Every president has also been a symbolic figure, an image of inspiration and pride to many people or the source of displeasure and despair for many others. Every president has left a mark on the history of this country. And every president, especially since the beginning of the twentieth century, has made a significant difference in the history of the world. Their powers are not absolute, nor are their choices unbounded, but the fact remains: presidents do matter.

The institution of the American presidency changes with each president. From the very beginning, the first four presidents shaped this institution because of the deliberate actions they took, the different roles they played, and the things they didn't do. George Washington wanted stability and continuation of the American political system. John Adams gave the system a test of partisanship and intolerance (consider the Alien and Sedition Acts, which in many ways limited political speech). Thomas Jefferson stimulated the body politic by encouraging broader public participation in government and a greater sense democracy. James Madison, through mistakes and inaction, tested the political system on its ability to survive. It survived.

Each president brought something new to the system, thus changing not only political institutions but also the lives of the citizens for generations to come. Each president was capable of projecting his own personality upon the most important decisions and policies of his time. James D. Barber distinguished two main personality features, two distinct sides in presidents that affected their historical impact.[2] The first is the rational one. Here the president calculates possible outcomes and chooses the best option. From the emotional side, however, the president acts upon his likes or dislikes. In addition, some presidents develop an individual propensity for innovation and change: they want to be active innovators involved in new policies and initiatives. Others play the role of caretaker, refraining from taking chances and preserving what has already been established or approved. In terms of rationality, there are *active* and *passive* presidents. In terms of emotionality, there are *positive* and *negative* presidents. For example, John Kennedy was active and positive. Richard Nixon was active and negative. Or, they may appear this way.

Presidents display their character traits and idiosyncrasies within particular historical circumstances. President Woodrow Wilson in 1919 demonstrated significant negativity when he failed to secure in the Senate U.S. membership in the League of Nations. His antipathy of the Republican

Senator Lodge was among the reasons why Wilson did not want to compromise. Wilson, though, was a diehard positive idealist: he was dreaming of a day when the world would be free of war and suffering. He believed that if he succeeded in the Senate with regard to the League of Nations, he could have opened the door to such a possibility.

Assuming that each presidential election is a mandate of sorts, the American people desire and expect their presidents to act in a certain way. Every president, then, enters the White House within a climate of specific expectations. There are high and low expectations, of course. The twentieth century reinforced the ability of presidents to effect images, to capture the imagination. We live in a consumer's society, and mass media allow presidents to "package" their policies in an attractive way to influence millions of people simultaneously. Two hundred years ago, presidents transformed society through policies and by changing institutions. Since then, the increasing influence of the media has given presidents the additional power to persuade and antagonize. In the television era, John Kennedy, as perhaps no other president before him, could inspire the imagination of many people in America and around the world. He was so universally popular that people in Communist Russia did not gloat when they learned about his assassination. They were shocked and saddened.

History may well look like a chain of presidential decisions. Each president considers choices, thinks, seeks advice, compares options, and chooses one decision over others. Everything appears simple in this scheme. You make the right decision and you get enough votes for reelection. Could President Hoover's willingness to use federal resources for massive direct relief programs during the Great Depression have saved his presidency? In the 1932 election, he carried only six states and lost badly. Could President Johnson have de-escalated the war in Vietnam in the mid-1960s? After he was elected in 1964, he wanted to negotiate with the Vietnamese ("anytime, anywhere"). The global situation was favorable, with increasing possibilities to end the war. In 1964, France, the United Nations, the Soviet Union, North Vietnam, and China all wanted to call an international peace conference on Vietnam. However, in February 1965, the military escalation began after an attack on the U.S. base in Pleiku, 240 miles south of Saigon. Johnson made a fateful decision to expand the war. He did not want to appear weak in front of his Republican opponents. He made his choice reluctantly. The war continued. Johnson, tired and disillusioned, decided not to run in 1968. The way each president handles crises reveals a lot about his individual personality.

During a crisis, weaknesses and strengths blend into a unique mold revealing an individual's traits that might otherwise remain hidden from direct observation. Learning how leaders handle crises is crucial in our understanding of history.

Do Elections Matter?

We often hear from our students that, theoretically, they like to study all those "close" elections, where "every vote counts." To them, it is entertaining to believe that a few votes here and there could have swayed the final vote. In reality, however, when we are dealing with national elections, everything is decided in advance, they say. So does this mean that the outcomes of our presidential races are already certain prior to elections?

It is true that, every now and then, elections amount to forgone conclusions: the electoral victories of George Washington in 1789 and 1792, Lyndon Johnson in 1964, Ronald Reagan in 1984, and Bill Clinton in 1996, for example, were never really in serious doubt. In modern elections national pollsters make scientific, statistically based forecasts of the outcomes weeks before Election Day and predict the winner. However, even the most sophisticated pollster is not able to predict the actual outcome. In the past, some electoral predictions based on opinion polls turned out incorrect. For example, in two almost classic cases—the 1948 U.S. presidential vote and the 1994 national elections in Great Britain—Harry Truman and John Major, respectively, were both projected to lose. Most commentators were certain about their defeat days in advance. The actual results proved them wrong. History shows a number of other examples of electoral "miracles" or "disasters" that demonstrated substantial changes in voters' actual decisions after they were polled ahead of the election. For instance, George H.W. Bush enjoyed very high approval ratings in 1991 at the end of the first Gulf war. He was well respected and widely regarded as a symbol of the victory in the Cold War. Yet he lost to the relatively unknown Governor Bill Clinton a year later.

More importantly, contrary to a current view that the close elections in 2000 and 2004 represent a new phase of American politics—a nation of voters deeply divided on the major issues on which elections focus—very close presidential elections have been common in the past. Looking at elections since 1824, fourteen of them have been decided by a margin of 5 percent or less! A few votes can and have changed history. Every vote counts.

Citizens in democratic societies have the right to vote. Thousands of people fought and died for this right on the barricades and in trenches, in revolutionary wars, and in battles for independence. We often hear that voting is one of the ultimate prizes in the struggle for freedom from tyranny, oppression, and autocracy. Yet in democratic countries, freedom to vote routinely comes together with freedom not to vote. When Americans elected John F. Kennedy president in 1960, the national turnout was nearly 63 percent. Three and a half decades later, in 1996, the turnout in the presidential election was already below 50 percent. Nonpresidential elections typically draw even lower numbers: voter turnout in the midterm congressional elections is commonly below 40 percent. In local elections, voter participation is consistently under 20 percent of registered voters and under 10 percent of eligible voters. Overall, turnout in U.S. presidential elections remains lower than in most other democracies in the world: the United States consistently ranks close to the bottom among over 170 democratic nations.[3]

People do not vote for a number of reasons. Surveys reveal at least two of the most important ones. The first one is the belief that a single vote does not change anything much in the electoral outcome: why do I have to vote if I know that my candidate will lose anyway? The other reason, as opinion polls show, is the belief that elections do not decide anything: no matter who is elected president, things will not change much.

Yet almost half of adults who did not make it to the polls in 2000—the closest presidential election in recent history—said they had regrets about not having participated.[4]

What Could Have Happened If . . . ?

"What if" scenarios refer to the past. They help us to appreciate the past's precious lessons.

What happened in the past appears even more significant in a historical context if we also explore what could have happened. In 1956, the White House Chief of Staff Sherman Adams told Vice President Nixon that it might be better if Nixon took a cabinet post rather than run again in 1956 for the vice presidency. Nixon, being very upset by this turn of events, seriously considered quitting government altogether. He felt he was underappreciated. If he had decided to resign, history would have probably written him off from its major accounting books. However, Nixon decided to carry on.

In considering historical events, most of us generally employ a two-dimensional approach. First, we look at things that have happened. We call this process *memory*. Second, based on those past events we tend to speculate and make predictions about the future. Looking back, we tend to focus on what actually happened (that is, the facts), but not on the possibile outcomes stemming from those events that failed to occur. In this book, however, we describe what has happened and what could have happened. We shift back and forth from interpreting the facts surrounding events that took place to analyzing related possibilities and decisions that didn't.

Historians like to study something that took place and can be confirmed. They are averse to theories that emphasize the impact of individuals on the course of events. Who knows what is happening within that "black box" of the human brain? In addition, there is a sense of inevitability in history. When our favorite team wins the Super Bowl, we say that we saw it coming. For some reason, in our view, what has happened in the past was destined to happen. However, most people recognize that when they think about the future, they can only guess. In our analysis, we support the view of Philip Tetlock and his colleagues who maintain that in history, many things that happened did not necessarily have to.[5] Of course, we are not in the position to give exact hindsight accounts about what might have happened. The degree of uncertainty is simply too high for a historian or political scientist to make forecasts. But many historians and political scientists are poets deep in their soul. And the poets love to mourn lost possibilities.

"What if" scenarios refer to the past. Yet all these "what ifs" help us to appreciate the prized urgency of now.

There are many who support the school of thought called *realism,* who say that from a policy standpoint, it is not that important who the president is. What is important is the country's national interest. They argue that, in the final analysis, the course of global relations is shaped not by the personal choices of leaders as individuals, but by the size, strength, and location of states. In this logic, for instance, it did not matter for the United States who was the Soviet leader in the 1940s. Stalin, as any other leader of the Soviet Union, would have been involved in a major competition and confrontation with the United States, because the two emerging superpowers had no choice but to engage in a struggle against each other.

We argue against such interpretations of history. Individual leaders do constantly exercise their individual choices and define their country's national interests accordingly. Do you think that if Al Gore were elected president in 2000 he would have defined national interest differently compared to George W. Bush's interpretations?

Individual choices affect electoral outcomes. Close presidential elections are among the most intriguing counterfactual history exercises. Many of us, especially after a personal setback, try to contemplate about what has happened and what went wrong. We typically ask the question: what could I have done to avoid that mistake? We do not have to wait for another unwanted event to start asking these questions again. We do the same in understanding politics.

In each case described in this book, we try to summarize and present the circumstances that best illustrate a particular election year. Then we look at the conditions that helped one candidate win a close contest against his opponent. We cite specific achievements of the victorious candidate and the shortcomings of the defeated opponent. Finally, we try to imagine what might have happened if the outcome of the election were different.

What This Book Will Not Examine

We try not to travel in the world of fantasy to imagine spectacular developments and unusual fairy-tale scenarios. Although a mystery novel would have been an interesting adventure to write, we will not try to exercise this choice. There are no suggestions here about unexpectedly surprising events such as a sudden discovery of a huge oil reserve in New York City that would have eliminated America's dependence on foreign oil in the 1960s. Nor do we fantasize about a scenario in which the Soviet leader Nikita Khrushchev was so disappointed about the victory of John Kennedy that he suffered a major stroke in 1961 that incapacitated him for years, which led to a sudden "thaw" in the Cold War. We assume that the Cuban missile crisis would have taken place and there was no magic dust to prevent the Berlin Wall from being erected overnight. We will not speculate about improbable scenarios such as Richard Nixon's sudden panic attack during the televised debates in 1960 or a decision by Fidel Castro to negotiate with Kennedy about a United States-Cuba reconciliation. We also assume that regardless of who was elected president of the United States, most major historic events would have happened anyway. France would have shopped around trying to sell Louisiana in 1803. The North Vietnamese government would not have stopped its guerilla operations in the South in the 1960s or later. In Iran, Ayatollah Khomeini would have come to power in Teheran regardless of who was the U.S. president at that time. Mikhail Gorbachev in the Soviet Union would certainly have been appointed secretary general if Walter Mondale, and not Ronald Reagan, were president of the United States.

All these suggest that in history, there are necessary and sufficient agents of change. Lyndon Johnson was a necessary agent to push forward with the civil rights legislations in the 1960s. However, without a favor-

able climate in Congress, without sufficient support in both parties, and
without a national civil rights movement led by Dr. Martin Luther King,
Jr., Johnson's legislative attempts would have been largely fruitless. Mikhail
Gorbachev was a necessary but not sufficient agent in the global political
changes after 1985. On the other side of the ocean, Ronald Reagan did
not foresee the end of the Cold War so soon. His toughness and firmness
in foreign policy was a combination of his beliefs rooted in the political
skills of George Shultz, the architect of U.S. foreign policy during the
1980s. Reagan was, in fact, a necessary actor who found himself in an
advantageous position because of his firm anti-Communism. He was
able to neutralize many of his hawkish staffers and approach the Soviet
Union from the position of dialogue and even accommodation. Had
Ronald Reagan been assassinated in 1981 and Vice President George
H.W. Bush had come to power, he would have been less likely to move
forward as rapidly as Reagan did. Bush would have relied mostly on his
rational thinking and intelligence rather than on political instincts.[6] In
terms of typology, Bush was a positive and passive president.

Many specific political outcomes are susceptible to the influence of
chance. Yet there is the *main line* of history, a chain of events that actually took place. Other events were insignificant to change the main line.
For example, World War I was, most likely, an inevitable event. No matter what might have happened before August 1914, the main line of
history led to the major conflict. In the same fashion, there is very little
chance that the United States would have chosen Germany and the Ottoman Empire as the main allies. During World War II, trapped in Berlin, Adolf Hitler could have, in theory, lasted a little bit longer than until
April 1945 and survived. Yet the United States would have developed
atomic weapons by the summer of that year. Hitler did not have such
weapons and did not have enough military and economic reserves to
continue the war. Germany would have lost the war anyway.

Finally, we have tried to avoid a temptation to fall under the magic
spell of "star" politicians and historic figures. We don't want to portray
possible outcomes and "what if" scenarios just to satisfy our nostalgic
thirst for something good that should have happened if history moved in

the direction we personally prefer. We are well aware that the notes of our emotions composed into a musical score by nostalgia, produce a sweet melody suitable probably for rosy fairy tales. In reality, our favorite "star" president can make as many mistakes as those whom we truly dislike.

What if Woodrow Wilson had lost the 1916 election? Some say that, almost certainly, America would have stayed out of World War I, and could have better used its immense wealth and power to secure a global and just peace in 1918 without firing a shot, without widowing a wife. We will argue against this "what if" scenario. This example refers to the past. Yet it might help us to appreciate the thrilling possibilities of tomorrow.

August 2008
Virginia

— 1 —

1800: THE ELECTION—A SECOND AMERICAN REVOLUTION?

The World and the Country

In 1800, when the Library of Congress was opening its doors in Washington, D.C., the population of the city was a little more than eight thousand people. The world's population in that year (the year of the discovery of infrared radiation and electrolysis of water) was approaching one billion, with seven million living in North America. Post-revolutionary France, under the rule of first consul Napoleon, was in the midst of war against England, Russia, and Austria. The kingdoms of Great Britain and Ireland merged, and their new flag, the Union Jack, was introduced. Great Britain dominated the seas as the world's strongest naval power, and was constantly challenged by the competing European states. It was the time of imperial expansions, formation of new nation-states, and popular challenges to old aristocratic authorities. The United States, meanwhile, was heading to its fourth presidential election.

For those who despair today over the negativity and length of modern presidential campaigns, the election of 1800 offers no consolation. A rematch of the 1796 election pitting President John Adams against Thomas Jefferson, the 1800 election was the culmination of years of factional strife between the Federalists and the Jeffersonian-Republicans.

ROOTS

Under the original Constitution electors in each state were to cast two votes for president, with only one of the votes going to an individual from the elector's state; the candidate receiving a majority of the votes was elected president and the candidate with the second highest total was awarded the vice presidency. By 1796 the factions had not yet jelled as parties capable of imposing discipline on the electors. Adams, the presidential candidate of the Federalists, received seventy-one electoral votes (a majority), but the party's obvious preference for vice president, Thomas Pinckney, garnered only forty-nine votes. Jefferson's sixty-eight electoral votes positioned him as the runner-up and hence the vice president-elect. Thus the two old friends, long since estranged, found themselves awkwardly coupled as president and vice president.

Jefferson's response in 1796 to second place rather than the grand prize was gracious and self-effacing. Outwardly he expressed no disappointment in his loss. On the contrary, he vowed to serve behind Adams. Perhaps reflecting on the warm relationship they had once had, Jefferson said of Adams, "I am his junior in life, was his junior in Congress, his junior in the diplomatic line, his junior lately in our civil government."[1] But his humble acceptance of the vice presidency masked the grave political differences between the two men. Moreover, four years of a divided executive branch did little to mend the differences. The gulf only widened and the animosity grew.

From his perch as vice president, Jefferson continued his opposition to the Federalists' policies. Through letters to friends, many of which were widely shared and even printed for public consumption, his financial support of writers critical of the Federalist party, and his masterful use of a network of what today would be called political operatives, Jefferson remained a vital force in the politics of the day.

Nevertheless, the first two years of the Adams' presidency were arduous for Jefferson as the Federalists' popularity surged. On assuming office in 1797, Adams inherited a looming crisis. France, at war with Great Britain, had become convinced that the recently concluded Jay Treaty signaled what they viewed as a dangerous rapport between Washington and London. In 1796, France proclaimed that it would not tolerate U.S. commerce with Great Britain. Even before Adams assumed the presidency, the French had seized some merchant ships and disrupted

U.S. trade. The situation became even more perilous when, only days after his inauguration, Adams learned that the French Provisional government had rebuffed a delegation sent to France by Washington. Angered by the snub, Adams, in his first speech to the new Congress, vehemently attacked the French and proposed a series of war preparedness measures, many of which were quickly passed.

Despite the bellicose language, Adams worked to resolve the problem diplomatically by sending a bipartisan team of negotiators to France. For months, the Quasi-War (frequently called the Undeclared War) with France languished on the periphery of American politics. It reemerged as a galvanizing issue in March 1798, however, when the negotiating team sent word that Talleyrand refused to see them. Even more incendiary, the negotiators reported that their French contacts had demanded bribes as a precondition to meeting Talleyrand. Although Adams seems to have contemplated asking for a declaration of war, publicly he was the voice of reason. He announced the failure of the negotiating team, but fearing that the full story would so incite the nation that he would have no option but war he did not release the text of the final message. Not ready to declare war but fearful that it was inevitable Adams asked Congress for increased defense expenditures and new taxes to cover the costs. Republicans were furious. Believing that the affair was a ploy by Federalists bent on war, they immediately demanded that Adams circulate the dispatches. Complying with their request, Adams redacted the names of the French agents who had demanded the bribes, naming them only X, Y, and Z, and released the communiqué.

Republicans overplayed their hand, as the XYZ Affair became a cause célèbre that elevated the fortunes of Adams and the Federalists. Everywhere Adams went during those days throngs of admirers greeted him. Suddenly he was heralded as a great leader; he was even favorably compared to his predecessor, George Washington. Never had Adams been so popular.

With war fever raging, the Federalists moved, under the cover of patriotism, to crush the opposition. Jefferson and his partisans were placed on the defensive, branded by the Federalists' press as traitors engaged in nefarious sedition. The vice president was frequently portrayed as an agent of France and a traitor to his own country. Worse yet, for the Republicans, the Federalists manipulated the fear of war and increased their control of Congress in the off-year elections of 1798, further marginalizing the Republicans. Fearful and pessimistic at times, Jefferson could only hope that the Federalists would overreach and create a backlash in public opinion.

The summer of 1798 belonged to Adams, however. At his request Congress created the Department of the Navy, funded a substantial growth in the number of warships available, upgraded coastal fortifications, and tripled the size of the army, all to be paid for by taxes on land, houses, and slaves. In its drive to prepare the nation for war and collect more taxes, Congress even passed its own version of the notorious British Stamp Act of 1765. But Congress went beyond what even Adams asked for, creating a temporary force known as the Provisional Army (sometimes referred to as the Additional Army) headed by George Washington, but in fact led by his hand-picked second in command, Alexander Hamilton. Jefferson could only stand by and watch as Hamilton, his archrival, became General Alexander Hamilton.

Once the military preparations were complete, Congress turned to the supposed internal threats. Arguing that enemies from within threatened the nation, Congress passed and President Adams, without comment, signed the infamous Alien and Sedition Acts. Under the acts, the president could deport aliens, and the period of residency required to become a citizen was raised from five to fourteen years. The Alien Act was clearly designed to strike at the heart of the Republicans as the party of choice for the new immigrants, particularly the Irish. As for sedition, Congress, relying on the old concept of seditious libel, made it a crime, punishable by a fine of as much as $5,000 and jail terms as long as five years, for anyone to publish or utter "any false, scandalous, and malicious" statement against the government of the United States or any of its officials.

Although the act allowed, as determined by the judge, the truth as a defense, the sweep of the law placed a powerful weapon in the hands of

Federalist judges. Suddenly Republican newspapers came under attack from the national government. Most of the prosecutions took place in Federalist-dominated northern states, but the acerbic James Callendar was imprisoned in Richmond for a treatise he wrote with the approval and financial support of Jefferson. All in all the government brought seventeen prosecutions, none of them against Federalist publishers and in only one case was the defendant found not guilty.

Alarmed by the acts, Jefferson and Madison reached out to the state governments with their famous Virginia-Kentucky Resolutions. Arguing that the national government contained only specific, enumerated powers, while all other powers resided with the states, the Resolutions called upon the states to nullify national laws that exceeded constitutional authority. Only Kentucky and Virginia acted on the resolutions, although the northern states passed resolutions condemning them. Nevertheless, as the war fever subsided, the draconian nature of the Alien and Sedition Acts created a public backlash that carried into the election year. Finally, Jefferson's hope that the Federalists would overreach took on some aspects of reality.

BEFORE THE 1800 ELECTION

While the 1796 election campaign lasted only 100 days, not starting until George Washington publicly announced his intention to forgo a third term, the 1800 run for the office was waged for more than a year. Contrary to modern practices, the campaign began long before either Adams or Jefferson officially declared their interests (although a rematch between Adam and Jefferson was assumed by most). Because the Constitution specifies that each state "Shall appoint, in such Manner as the Legislature therefore may direct, a Number of Electors, equal to the whole Number of Senators and Representatives to which the State may be entitled in Congress," the battle for the presidency began in the state assemblies.

As all involved understood, the presidential election was to be decided by local elections in a handful of states. There was, in 1799, no settled practice for selecting electors. Going into the presidential election campaign eight states provided that the state legislature would appoint the electors.[2] In five states the electors were selected by voters divided into districts, and the remaining three states provided for statewide election of the electors.[3] In some key states the presidential election hung on how the electors were to be chosen.

In Virginia, for instance, the Republicans changed their method of selecting electors as early as January 1799. Originally Jefferson favored district elections (the method used by the state in 1796) as the most democratic means of providing a check against an elitist Electoral College. As the 1800 election approached, however, he had a change of heart. Arguing that it weakened a state's power to cast a divided electoral vote when a majority of the states produced unified slates of electors (by either legislative selection or a statewide election), Jefferson urged Virginia's governor, James Monroe, to press for a bill converting to statewide election.[4] After a bitter fight, the Virginia legislature, although controlled by Jeffersonian Republicans, narrowly approved a bill to abolish the district voting and replace it with a statewide election system. It may be that Jefferson's transformation on this issue was dictated by his concern that Virginia's electoral clout not be diminished, but it is also true that he had been embarrassed in 1796 by a Virginia elector who cast a vote for Adams. His new position guaranteed that a Virginia Federalist would not be among the electors in 1800.

In Pennsylvania, the politics of electors' selection were reversed. In 1796, the Federalists had enacted a statewide election of the electors, believing that this would ensure that all of the states' electoral votes would go to Adams. As sometimes happens, however, the plan backfired. Jefferson won all but one of the states' electoral votes. Not surprisingly then, as the 1800 election approached, the Federalists advocated either district elections or legislative selection. Their ability to enact either plan turned on the state elections of 1799, particularly the contest for Pennsylvania governor. As the Federalists well understood, a Republican governor would veto any plan favorable to the Federalists. Thus the gubernatorial election took on added importance. Republicans and Federalists alike thought that the fate of the presidential election hinged on this one gubernatorial election. In the end, after a bitter struggle, the Republican candidate, Thomas McKean, won the race for governor by 5,000 votes out of 70,000 cast.[5] Additionally, the Republicans gained control of the lower house and nearly took the State Senate. This left Pennsylvania in a difficult position. It had no means of selecting the electors (the procedure used in 1796 was authorized only for that election), and the state was left with a divided government that promised nothing but stalemate.

Surprisingly, however, it was New York, a state assumed to be a Federalist stronghold, that created the greatest ripples. New York's legislature selected the electors, and in 1796 all twelve electoral votes had gone to Adams. But the legislative elections in April 1800 constituted a bitter pill for the Federalists as they unexpectedly lost control of the New York legislature. What happened to the Federalists that year is simple—they were out-organized in New York City. Republicans emerged victorious mainly because Aaron Burr, former U.S. senator and a powerful member of the New York state legislature, built a very strong campaign organization that overwhelmed the Federalists. Burr was cunning, strategic, and relentless in his pursuit of electoral victory in New York City's poorer neighborhoods. Exploiting the image of the Federalist as the party of the rich and the enemy of the poor, particularly the enemy of newly arrived immigrants, New York Republicans inflamed class politics. More importantly, Burr channeled these passions into political action. Presaging modern political campaigns, Burr collected and organized information on every possible voter. His meticulous records contained names, addresses, occupations, and the political leanings of everyone in the contested wards of New York City. Turning his own home into Republican campaign headquarters, Burr dispatched party workers to visit every likely Republican supporter—encouraging them to vote and instructing them on how to cast their ballot. Unheard of at the time, Burr created a campaign based on door-to-door canvassing—even providing German speakers for the newly arrived immigrants. For those that might have trouble getting to the polls, Burr made sure that they had transportation to and from the voting places. Additionally, Burr personally addressed crowds urging them to vote Republican. To top it off, Burr recruited an extraordinarily prestigious slate of Republican candidates—men of revolutionary war fame. Never mind that several of the candidates were too old to serve effectively; they had, as we would say now, "high name recognition."

When the dust had settled, the Republicans had taken every contested seat in New York City. Impressive in itself, the victory in New York City reverberated throughout the state, and even the nation. Suddenly, what had been a Federalist-dominated legislature became a Republican legislative body. More importantly, it became a Republican legislature with the power to select all twelve of New York's electors. As Burr said to his Federalist rivals, "We have beat you by superior Management."[6]

A great malaise swept across the Federalists. While back in 1796 Jefferson had polled no electoral vote north of the Mason-Dixon line except those in Pennsylvania, the Republicans were now guaranteed twelve votes from New York. No one felt this more keenly than Alexander Hamilton. Hamilton's first response to the loss was to propose that New York's governor, John Jay, call a special session of the New York Assembly while it was still subject to Federalist control. A special legislative session, if successful, would allow the Federalists to alter the New York law and require that presidential electors be chosen by district elections—a plan that would have guaranteed the Federalists a majority of the electoral votes. Governor Jay refused to engage in an obvious partisan ploy and New York was lost to the Federalists.

Ironically, the loss of New York forced Hamilton to back Adams' candidacy. Hamilton's distaste for Adams was certainly not a secret, but without Adams on the ticket, the Federalists risked losing votes in New England, votes they could no longer spare. As soon as the New York results were clear, Hamilton sent a message to the members of the Federalist caucus meeting in Philadelphia imploring them to nominate Adams. A few members of the caucus had openly flirted with the idea of replacing Adams with Chief Justice Ellsworth, but with the loss of New York and Hamilton's plea, the caucus members seemingly lost their interest in such a bold move.

With the Adams nomination decided, the remaining issue was to select the second nominee. Again, the caucus largely acceded to Hamilton's urgings and selected C. C. Pinckney of South Carolina. Although Pinckney was a man of distinction, his major appeal was that as a member of an old and powerful South Carolina family he might be able to garner some southern support—support that the Federalists desperately needed if they were going to hold onto the White House. Although it was widely understood that as the incumbent Adams was the Federalist nominee for president and that Pinckney was the vice presidential nominee, the caucus made no such distinction. In putting forward the two candidates, the Federalists simply urged electors to support both for president. Again, Hamilton's influence was clearly felt during the nomination process. His hope was that both Adams and Pinckney would carry the Federalists' strongholds, while Pinckney would be the second choice, behind Jefferson, of some southern electors. In this way, overall the majority of votes might go to Pinckney.

Meeting a few days after the Federalists, the Republicans nominated Jefferson and Burr, a repeat of the 1796 ticket. Unlike the Federalists, however, the Republicans made it clear that Jefferson was the presidential nominee.

Results of the 1800 Presidential Election

Part I

With the candidates known, the election campaign began in earnest that spring. It was the custom that the candidates avoided public campaigning. However, behind the scenes, Adams and Jefferson were actively corresponding with supporters, suggesting tactics and coordinating their campaigns in the states. More important, their surrogates in the press were exceedingly busy. As waged in the press, the campaign was awash in vilification and slander. Republican newspapers routinely characterized Adams as a person holding monarchical tendencies, a would-be dictator determined to install a hereditary throne. Adams was also frequently portrayed as too old (he was sixty-five by the time of the election) and feeble for the presidential job—although not too old, according to one baseless account, to have dispatched a frigate to England to bring back mistresses for his amusement. More broadly, the Republicans portrayed the entire Federalist Party as interested only in the welfare of the merchants and traders—who were driven by the desire for monetary gain. Blinded, their rivals charged, by their affection for Great Britain, the Federalists were fixated on restoring the policies that the British had used to oppress the colonists. The large national debt and the new taxes that the Federalists had instituted were a constant source of condemnation.

Giving at least as good as they got, the Federalists described Jefferson as a dangerous revolutionary captivated by French philosophy and morals intent on bringing the nation to a state of revolutionary chaos. Jefferson, the Federalists charged, was the American Jacobean determined to destroy the country's social order. Moreover, the Federalists assailed Jefferson for his religious beliefs—or, more correctly, they said for his lack of belief. Not only was Jefferson depicted as an atheist, but he also was assumed to be committed to the total obliteration of religion in American life. New Englanders were warned to hide their Bibles less Jefferson find and burn them. In Federalist-backed newspapers and from pulpits across New England, voters were warned that the election of Jefferson would bring God's wrath upon the nation.

Throughout the summer and fall, rumors of the likely electoral outcomes proliferated. Since the New York elections, few observers gave Adams much of a chance. The question seemed to be if it would be Jefferson and Burr or Pinckney and Jefferson. When results of the October legislative elections in South Carolina finally made their way north, Adams himself concluded that it would be Pinckney and Jefferson, with Jefferson serving a second term as vice president. As for Jefferson, he had assumed for some time that Adams was not his rival. By his calculations, he had the best chance of garnering a majority, but there was a chance that Pinckney could best him. According to Jefferson's predictions, the election was in the hands of South Carolina.

As Election Day—December 3, 1800— approached, the news from

the states continued to predict alternative outcomes. Jefferson had hoped to secure some votes from Rhode Island, but by Election Day, this outcome seemed unlikely. Conversely, on December 2, word that Pennsylvania legislators had reached an accord that would allow the appointment of eight electors for Jefferson and seven for Adams cheered the Republican candidate. This was fewer votes than Jefferson had received from Pennsylvania in 1796, but combined with the New York votes, it was more votes north of the Mason-Dixon than he had in his previous run. Still, the question remained: would the South Carolina electors give their second vote to Pinckney?

Ballots cast in December could not be opened or counted until February 11, 1801; but by Christmas of 1800 newspapers were reporting a victory for Jefferson. The Republican press, based on reports from the various states, was proclaiming Jefferson the next president. Because the Republicans had specified that Jefferson was their presidential candidate, most ignored the fact that projections had Jefferson and Burr tied at seventy-three votes each. Jefferson had always assumed that Georgia electors would withhold one or two votes from Burr, and rumors had it that at least one South Carolina voter had withheld his vote for Burr, but the unofficial counts confirmed that this had not happened.

Despite the Republicans' designation of Jefferson as their presidential candidate, the tie between the two candidates presented problems. Under the U.S. Constitution, if more than one candidate has a majority of the electoral vote and they have the same number of votes, the House of Representatives shall immediately convene to choose the president. In doing so, each state is to have one vote with a majority of states being necessary to produce the winner. The problem for the Republicans was that Federalists controlled the House. It is true that the Republicans controlled more state delegations than the Federalists, but they did not have the majority of state delegations needed to elect Jefferson. Having captured a majority of the electoral vote, Jefferson now found his fate in the hands of the Federalists.

Jefferson immediately appealed to Burr suggesting that he renounce any interest in the presidency. In exchange, Jefferson promised to make

Burr a powerful vice president. Burr's response was evasive, but he seemed committed to serving as the vice president. But that was before Christmas when Burr thought that a Vermont elector had given his second vote to Jefferson, thus avoiding a tie. By early January, Burr had learned that the vote was indeed tied, and consequently he let it be known that he was also a candidate for the top job. Although Burr never publicly revealed his desire, word spread quickly that he intended to fight for the presidency.

PART II

From January to February, Republicans debated their prospects and a divided Federalist Party sought agreement on their response to the electoral tie. There seemed no way to avoid the need for a decision by the House. This was confirmed on February 11 when Jefferson, as president of the Senate, opened the electoral ballots and read out the votes, state by state, concluding by announcing the totals as: seventy-three for Jefferson; seventy-three for Burr; sixty-five for Adams; sixty-four for Pinckney; and one for John Jay. The only remarkable moment came when Jefferson opened the ballots from Georgia and noticed that they had not been completed correctly. Nevertheless, Jefferson announced four votes for himself and four for Burr.

With the final vote total now official, the House of Representatives immediately withdrew to deliberate and vote to break the tie. The first vote taken produced eight votes for Jefferson (one state, one vote), one shy of the majority needed. Burr received six votes, all from Federalist-dominated states. Two states, Maryland and Vermont, were deadlocked. Before the day was over, the House would vote again, and again, and again. It was done fifteen times, but the result did not change. In fact, through thirty-five votes, the vote total stayed the same. Finally, on February 17, the stalemate was broken with the thirty-sixth vote. After receiving assurances that Jefferson would accept certain terms demanded by the Federalists, the lone representative from Delaware, James Bayard, abstained. This single abstention by a thirty-three-year-old representative from Delaware was enough to put Jefferson in the White House. His actions cascaded, however, as the Federalist delegation from South Carolina declined to vote. Since there were no Republican representatives from South Carolina this amounted to another state abstaining. Additionally, none of the Federalists from Maryland or Vermont voted, moving those states from deadlocked to Jefferson. Altogether, that meant that finally, the House produced a winner. Jefferson was elected with the support of ten states.

Jefferson: How He Could Have Lost the 1800 Election

Jefferson described the election of 1800 as the second American Revolution every bit as important as the first. This strikes most as the kind of hyperbole typical of Jefferson. There is no doubt that the 1800 election was crucial in many respects, however. With hindsight this election is generally seen as the product of the first political party system. There is some truth to this, but in 1800 the Federalists and Republicans were more prototypes of parties than actual parties. What makes the election of 1800 momentous is that a new, struggling nation accepted the legitimacy of a leadership change produced by a hotly contested and closely matched election. There was no coup, no secessionist movement, nor riots or armed revolts. Instead, the election results were largely, if begrudgingly, accepted and a peaceful transition of power occurred. Very few countries can find similar examples in their history.

Nothing about this peaceful transition was assured, however. There were several likely outcomes that could have produced resistance and even violent reactions.

No Result

One strategy available to the Federalists was to take no action, or at least no action that would resolve the contest between Jefferson and Burr. What would this mean? With certainty, on March 4, the last day of the Adams administration, the constitutional provision covering succession would have taken effect. Assuming that the divided Senate Federalists could elect a president pro tempore of the Senate (the highest-ranking senator), that individual would act in place of an elected president until the new Congress convened, late in 1801. Should the Senate be unable to elect a president pro tempore, the office would fall to the Speaker of the House. In either case, the acting president would be unelected, and he would have been a Federalist.

Madison fearing such a tactic, proposed that on March 4 Jefferson and Burr jointly call the new Congress into special session to resolve the dispute. Of course, the constitutionality of such a move was highly questionable and most certainly would have occasioned a constitutional crisis for the young republic.

BURR WINS

Given that Jefferson and Burr were tied in the electoral vote, Burr appeared to be Jefferson's most serious rival. Certainly, Jefferson was worried about Burr. Although, back in December 1800, Burr had pledged to accept his role as the vice president, several weeks passed without a public announcement from him declining any interest in the top job. Burr could have severely undercut the Federalists by simply refusing to accept the presidency. Notably he remained silent, however. Jefferson grew increasingly suspicious that Burr was trying to negotiate his way to the presidency.

Many Federalists felt that the office was Burr's for the asking. He needed only to satisfy certain conditions. Rumors swirled of bribes being offered to swing the necessary votes. But Burr's chances of winning were not so obvious. It was not the Federalists who would have to change, it was the Republicans. As the first and subsequent votes stood, Burr had six states, Jefferson eight, and two states, Maryland and Vermont, were evenly divided. To win, Burr needed to move some Republican votes. This was not impossible, but the odds were long. There were four delegations from which Burr could have picked up enough Republican votes to win, but he would have to carry at least three of the four states to beat Jefferson. However, Jefferson needed only one vote, which could have come from Maryland, Vermont, or Delaware to give him the majority.

Clearly Burr's odds were long and the costs high. His problem was simple. If he made a move to secure the votes he needed to win, losing would end his career. Even the slightest effort to take the office away from Jefferson would destroy any chances of Burr having a future in the Republican Party. The same could be said of any Republican congressman who supported him. They would all be pariahs in the party. Just what Burr was thinking remains unclear, but it may be that he was thinking of his future. He was certainly young enough (in February 1801 he turned forty-four) that he could be a viable candidate even eight years later. However, for that to happen he would need the solid backing of the southern Republicans. That was something he could never have if he was seen as trying to take the presidency away from Jefferson.

Unfortunately for Burr, he did nothing. His inaction cost him future support in the party and he lost whatever opportunity he had to grab the presidency in 1800.

ADAMS IS ELECTED

Often lost in hubbub surrounding the Jefferson-Burr tie and subsequent maneuverings in the House, is the fact that Adams actually polled better in some places than he had in 1796. It is true that Adams collected only sixty-five electoral votes in 1800 compared to his seventy-one in 1796, but in the South, Adams actually increased his vote total in 1800. Moreover, the last-minute compromise in Pennsylvania gave him additional votes from that state. Unfortunately, for Adams these gains could not offset his narrow loss of the New York legislature. In 1796, all twelve of New York's electoral votes went to Adams, but in 1800, all twelve went to Jefferson and Burr. Had the Federalists not been out-organized by Burr in New York City, where the Republicans won four of seven wards by very thin margins, or had the lame-duck Federalist legislature of New York altered the rules on selecting electors creating a district-based election system, Adams would have polled more votes than Jefferson. Alternatively, if Virginia had not eliminated its district elections in favor of a statewide election, Adams may well have picked up enough votes in that state to have defeated Jefferson.

Adams' loss also owes a great deal to the original Constitution's provision regarding apportioning seats in the House. Under the three-fifths compromise reached in 1787, in a state, five slaves (who couldn't vote) counted as three free persons for enumeration purposes. Without the three-fifths compromise, Jefferson's base would not have been large enough to overcome Adams. The Electoral College majority would have belonged to Adams.

The only other way that Adams could have won would have been if the House excluded the electoral votes from Georgia. As you remember, although Jefferson had counted the votes, the electors did not sign them and thus they were technically flawed. If the House had invalidated the Georgia votes, the Federalists could have argued that no candidate had a majority of the appointed electors, as the Constitution required. Lacking a majority, the top five candidates would be referred to the House. Although possible, this tactic had little chance of securing the election for Adams. First of all, the House had no procedures to challenge votes, and it would have taken months of intense debate to put any in place. Second, the Federalist interpretation that no majority candidate existed if the Georgia votes were disallowed was highly arguable. The Constitution requires a majority of the electors appointed. The Federalist argument hinged on the assumption that even though the Georgia votes would not be counted, their electors would be considered appointed. Obviously, this was not an interpretation that the Republicans would have accepted. Finally, even if the Federalists had somehow navigated through these procedural difficulties, they did not control enough state delegations to deliver the election for Adams.

Political difficulties aside, this tactic would most likely have provoked violence. Pennsylvania had already publicly warned that its state militia was positioned to invade Washington should the Federalists deny Republicans the presidency. Jefferson had delivered a similar warning to Adams. There would have been no peaceful transition of power. The election of Adams by the Congress would have sparked insurrection.

If Jefferson Were Not Elected

Assessing how the nation would have differed if Jefferson had lost in 1800 is especially complicated because it is difficult to sort out Jefferson's deeds and words. In his inaugural address, Jefferson famously said, "We are all Republicans, we are all Federalists." As if to prove the point, President Jefferson often acted like a Federalist even as he espoused Republican principles. As Hamilton predicted, President Jefferson was not the radical that Federalists had assumed.

RESTORING FREEDOM

One of Jefferson's first acts as president was to pardon those convicted under the Alien and Sedition Acts. Then, with Jefferson's apparent approval, Congress allowed the acts to expire in 1801 and 1802. A Republican-dominated Congress, at Jefferson's urging, also replaced the 1798 Naturalization Act, which required fourteen years of residency for citizenship. The 1802 act required only five years of residence, acceptance of the Constitution, and the renunciation of foreign allegiance.

These are actions that would have been difficult for Adams. Although Adams' personal enthusiasm for prosecuting his political rivals seemingly waned by 1800, it is unlikely that he would have pardoned those who had been jailed for attacking him. Moreover, he most likely would have opposed the changes in immigration policy. Easing immigration rules was a policy that disadvantaged the Federalist Party, since the Republicans were far better at recruiting new immigrants into their party than were the Federalists.

THE LOUISIANA PURCHASE

As every school-aged child knows, President Jefferson doubled the size of the country with the 1803 Louisiana Purchase from France. Would Adams have done the same? Obviously it is impossible to speculate on what Adams may have thought in advance about this expansive move. Ironically, Jefferson's actions here completed Hamilton's dream. As commander of the Provisional army, Hamilton had often talked of using military force to expand into the very areas that Jefferson purchased, but there is no evidence that Adams shared this vision. Whatever Adams may have desired, it seems unlikely that Adams would have been able to make the purchase, however.

There was great public pressure, fueled by the Federalists, to remove the French bottleneck to American trade. Indeed, Jefferson contemplated war as a means of securing the territory. But when the opportunity arose, Jefferson anguished over whether he had the legal power to acquire the land, even considering a constitutional amendment to empower him. In the end, Jefferson convinced himself that the purchase was within the implied powers of the president as a means of protecting the nation from the perceived threat from Napoleon's France. The key problem for Adams, though, would have been a hostile Republican Congress. The Republican Congress may well have characterized the deal as another example of the Federalists' monarchial—and very expensive—grasp of power. If Adams had done the same, Republicans also would have undoubtedly characterized the whole scheme as a further enrichment of the wealthy. In other words, political opposition to the Louisiana Purchase would have been so fierce, that it would have discouraged Adams from even trying it. In modern terms, we might characterize this as a predecessor to the saying, "only Nixon could go to China," which means that political leaders from one political camp can implement policies that their political opponents cannot, and vice versa.

In the end, Jefferson fulfilled Hamilton's dream, but at the same time ensured that the agrarian Republic he so idealized would continue. The purchase made enormous lands available for cultivation, but it also built a vast commercial network—a very Hamiltonian goal.

Taxes and Spending

One of the hallmarks of Jefferson's presidency was his ability, despite the fifteen million dollars that he spent acquiring the Louisiana territory, to bring spending under control. His cabinet appointments worked hard to cut government expenditures. Among other money-saving actions, the secretary of the treasury cut the Army budget in half and Jefferson closed some diplomatic missions overseas. Along with the spending cuts, the Jefferson administration cut taxes. In fact, it eliminated all internal taxes, including the much-hated 1791 Whiskey Tax (which included taxes on distilled spirits and carriages).

Revenue to fund government operations came largely from taxes on imports and the sale of public lands—the scale of which was increased as a result of the Louisiana Purchase.

With or without Jefferson, much of this would have happened anyway, even with Adams in the White House. The difference would have been that a Republican-dominated Congress would have led by passing various bills. The Whiskey Tax, for instance, was extremely unpopular, even among Federalists. As President Adams may have tempered the cost-cutting programs, Republicans were united on the need to rein in spending and reduce taxes.

DEMOCRATIZATION

Symbolically Jefferson signaled the beginning of a new, more democratic era in American society and government. He eschewed many of the trappings of office, most established by President Washington. Jefferson's dress was plainer and his customs far less formal than those associated with the more aristocratic Federalists.

Symbolism aside, Jefferson's election did in important ways lead the way to a more democratic society and political system in the United States. Jefferson's electoral success was founded on organizing citizens to action. It was after all Burr's superior abilities to unite and energize ordinary people that placed New York in the Jefferson column and thus in the White House. Federalists who had long believed in government by the best were beaten by a political campaign taken to the people. By 1804, what had earlier been unthinkable to Federalists—treating voters as their equals—was accepted as a political necessity even by the Federalists. With hindsight, it is obvious that democratization of the American political system was inevitable, but most likely an Adams victory would have slowed its advancement.

Conclusion

It is common to talk of presidential elections as critical to the nation's development, its political institutions and policies, and the lives of its people. Without a doubt, the fate of the nation is frequently said to hang on the electoral outcome. Although these judgments are often inflated, even sensationalized in most extravagant ways to create interest, the election of 1800 truly was a crucial moment in American history. Over two hundred years later it may be difficult to understand for contemporary readers how close the Constitution came to failing. Only the second contested election in the nation's history, the election of 1800 brought the nation to the brink of disaster.

Despite the impassioned debates and the disputed outcome, the nation passed the crucial test: power was passed from one set of rulers to another. Most importantly and amazingly, the transfer occurred without violence. History will reveal so many examples from so many countries when this was not the case.

Just as importantly, the election of 1800 hinged on a handful of votes. Federalists often castigated Jefferson as the president who achieved office on the "backs of slaves." It is certainly true that without the added representation that the three-fifths compromise gave to the southern states, Jefferson would not have been elected. But the Federalists were overlooking the importance of the average citizen's electoral behavior. Even with the overrepresentation of the southern states, the Federalists could have and should have won the election. Their Achilles heel, their most sensitive liability as a party, was their disdain for the common people of New York. A small number of votes in the city of New York sealed Adams' fate. He desperately needed New York to hold on to office, but the Federalists were simply out-organized. Burr was clearly a genius at political organizing, but the fact is the Federalists were hard-pressed to appeal directly to those who they thought to be inferior. Of course, there is irony in this. Jefferson, the spokesman for the agricultural Republic, owed his election to a small number of working class and poor voters in New York City, that least of agrarian localities.

— 2 —

1876: HAYES DEFEATS TILDEN—
A COMMISSION DECIDES

1876: The Election Year

THE WORLD AND THE COUNTRY

The 1870s was, for many countries including the United States, a period of rapid urban and industrial development marked by improving living standards, expanding political rights, and growing nationalism. In Europe, the unified German Empire eagerly sought expansion and domination while France was recovering from its humiliating defeat to Prussia. The Russian Empire was growing but already cracking under mounting internal political pressures. The Ottoman Empire was also crumbling under the persistent attacks of nationalist forces, especially in Greece and the Balkans. Unlike Russia and the Ottomans, Japan was abolishing its traditional feudal system while establishing many western-like legal and government institutions. The country of the rising sun was about to enter an era of global competition.

In many respects, 1876 was a glorious year for the United States. Across the country, in every city and village, Americans were celebrating the nation's centennial. Of course the foremost celebration was being held in Philadelphia, the city where it all began. Philadelphia's Centennial Exhibition was the first world's fair held in the United States. With over two hundred buildings visited by more than ten million people, the Centennial Exhibition constituted a watershed moment in American history. Focused as it was on technology and progress, the Exhibition showcased American ingenuity with, among other things, a slice of the cable that would be used to construct the Brooklyn Bridge, and the first type-writer and telephone. But it was the giant 1500 horsepower Corliss Steam Engine, started to great fanfare by President Ulysses S. Grant and Emperor Dom Pedro of Brazil, that captivated the visitors and announced to the world that the United States was emerging as a leader in technology. It was the year of the first telephone call, the formation of Major League Baseball, as well as the founding of Johns Hopkins and Texas A&M universities.

Politically, the centennial year was one of turmoil and danger, however. As the year progressed, the nation experienced a presidential election like none it had ever seen before. Charges of fraud, intimidation, vote stealing, and in the end, a controversial choice among the candidates, divided the nation and left even the winner crippled and ineffectual.

Only four years earlier, the Republican Party had seemed invincible. In 1872 Grant had been reelected by a substantial majority of the electorate. However, the Republicans had been stung by an internal revolt that led to the creation of a group known as the Liberal Republicans—a group that proved to be an electoral nuisance for the party. For their candidate, the Liberal Republicans endorsed the sixty-one-year-old Democratic candidate, Horace Greeley. An anomalous man of strong views on issues from vegetarianism to socialism, both of which he favored, Greeley turned out to be a dreadful candidate who wilted in the face of Republican attacks.

Grant's easy reelection victory cheered Republicans, but the joy was not to last. During the campaign a scattering of stories about corruption reaching into the administration appeared, but they had little influence on the electorate. The essence of the stories was that Credit Mobilier, the company that built the transcontinental railway and was owned by officials of Union Pacific, had distributed over nine million dollars in stock as payoffs to government officials, including Vice President Schuyler Cox, Secretary of the Treasury George S. Boutwell, and several members of Congress.

Credit Mobilier was the first, but not the last, scandal to tar the second Grant administration, however. The administration continued to be buffeted by scandals, big and small. In 1875 the famous Whiskey Ring affair led investigators to one of Grant's most trusted aides. Grant's own secretary of the treasury, Benjamin H. Bristow, ordered raids on distillers and the offices of U.S. tax collectors in three different cities. (Grant never forgave Bristow for the raids.) Allegedly, the distillers in collusion with tax collectors defrauded the government out of millions in unpaid tax revenues. Moreover, the investigators charged that Colonel Orville Babcock, the president's personal secretary, had tipped off one of the tax collectors to the upcoming raids. Babcock was never convicted, but Grant was forced to reassign him to a far less visible government post—inspecting lighthouses.

Just as this scandal was fading the administration was rocked by another one involving the secretary of war, William Worth Belknap. The secretary was accused of accepting kickbacks from the operator of the Fort Sill post store in Oklahoma—the only store allotted, due to Belknap's intervention, to supply the nearby Indian tribes. In response to the news, the House voted articles of impeachment against Belknap and he immediately resigned, leading the Senate, by a narrow margin, to drop the charges.

Scandals were only part of the problem, however. Although Grant had been reelected partly on the basis of a strong economy, the good times ended abruptly in 1873. For years Americans had depended on Europeans to purchase their securities, but in May 1873, massive panic hit the Vienna markets. Austrians and Europeans began to restrict their purchase of American securities and even sell off what they owned. Without European money, the American market could no longer support the demands for credit. The strains led in September 1873 to the bankruptcy of Jay Cooke and Company—the financiers of the Northern Pacific Railway. Then, one after another, banks began to close, and the panic turned into a depression.

Furthering the Republican's troubles were the actions of the Republican-dominated Forty-second Congress. As the Congress was about to adjourn, and just months before the markets crashed, its members voted sizable raises for government officials, including senators and representatives. Congressional salaries rose $2,500 retroactively. This so-called Salary Grab infuriated the public just as the congressional elections of 1874 were kicking off.

Scandals, economic crisis, the Salary Grab, and a growing disenchantment by northerners with post-Civil War Reconstruction policies created a Republican electoral disaster in the 1874 congressional elections. Republicans had expected to lose some seats, but nothing like what actually happened. When the votes were finally tallied, the Republicans lost ninety-six seats in the House and eight in the Senate. For the first time since the Civil War, Democrats found themselves in control of the House. They wasted little time, serving notice of their power on Grant. The first order of business for the new Congress was passing a resolution warning the president that a third term would be "unwise, unpatriotic, and fraught with peril to our free institutions."[1]

Most importantly, the elections of 1874 signaled that the Republicans were facing a new reality. Greeley's 1872 attacks on the Republicans had not garnered him many votes, but they had set the stage for a rising Democrat party. What had not resonated in 1872 was beginning to gain political traction as 1876 approached.

BEFORE THE ELECTION

At the beginning of 1876 the nomination seemed to belong to James Blaine, a forty-six-year-old Congressman from Maine. He had served fourteen years in the House, and during the Grant administration, he had been an accomplished and widely admired Speaker of the House. A flamboyant and eloquent politician, he had distinguished himself by his ability to build consensus. Blaine had also demonstrated a tendency to support most but not all of the Radical Republicans' concerns (they demanded, for example, a more radical approach to dismantle the political legacy of the defeated Confederacy). Once the Democrats took over the House, however, Blaine put away his coalition-building style and became a vocal critic of Democrats.

Blaine's strategy for gaining the nomination was by now a tried and true approach to winning. Democrats could not be trusted because they

sympathized with the South during the Civil War. Blaine seemed un-
beatable. Only three other candidates appeared to have a chance of winning the nomination: New York Senator Roscoe Conkling; Benjamin
Bristow, the man who prosecuted the Whiskey Ring; and Indiana Senator Oliver Perry Morton. Topping the list of second tier candidates was
Ohio Governor Rutherford B. Hayes.

As many a candidate has learned, being the front-runner and being
selected are not one in the same. On his way to the nomination, Blaine
became the target of a congressional investigation. As part of a complicated stock scheme, Blaine was accused of buying back worthless stock
that he had sold to friends with money he borrowed from the president
of the Union Pacific Railroad—the note was never called in. Blaine was
never convicted of any crime nor did his colleagues censure him. Nevertheless, coming just days before the start of the Republican nominating
convention, the charges damaged him. To his foes in the Republican
Party, this was proof that he was unfit for the nomination. For other
Republicans, knowing that corruption was going to be a major Democratic issue in the general election, it was a good reason to reconsider
their support for Blaine.

Even with his reputation damaged, Blaine remained a powerful
political force. At the end of the first round of voting, Blaine was short of
a majority but well ahead of his nearest competitor. At this point Hayes
was in fifth place with sixty-one votes—well shy of the 379 needed to
secure the nomination. Successive rounds of voting produced little change.
Then in the fifth round, the Michigan delegation switched its votes from
Blaine to Hayes, and the delegates began to sense that a change was happening. At the end of the fifth ballot, Hayes was in third place, but still
no majority existed. Not until the seventh ballot did the convention ar-
rive at a decision. The final round of voting began with a couple of dozen
votes shifting to Blaine. Then came the votes from Indiana, where the
head of the delegation announced that their favorite son candidate, Oliver
Morton, was withdrawing from consideration and that the bulk of the
state's votes were cast for Hayes. Then, one by one, the remaining candidates dropped out, throwing the majority of their votes to Hayes. John

Harlan of Kentucky announced that Benjamin Bristow was withdrawing from the race. That meant twenty-four additional votes for Hayes.
Finally, the roll call came to New York. There the head of the delegation
revealed that Roscoe Conkling had decided to withdraw, shifting a set of
sixty-one votes to Hayes. When the roll call was completed, Hayes was
declared the winner. The margin was five votes.

Dramatic as the floor vote was, what played out on that seventh
ballot was a plan that had been hatched on the first night of the convention. On that first evening, Edward Noyes, the campaign manager for
Hayes, had reached an agreement with representatives of the Morton
and Bristow campaigns. They agreed that their candidates would test the
waters for a few ballots and then if their chances did not look good,
throw their support to Hayes. The deal with the Bristow camp involved
a promise to nominate Bristow's friend and campaign manager John
Harlan for the Supreme Court.

In the end, fifty-three-year-old Hayes won the nomination as
the least objectionable candidate. His followers were few, but he had
the advantage of having few detractors. He was everyone's second
choice.

Democrats heading off to St. Louis for the party convention were
in a joyous mood. After all, the congressional elections of 1874 had been
a triumph for them, all but three southern states had been redeemed
(released from carpet-bag rule), the economy was in dire straights, and
there seemed no end to the constant stream of scandals coming out of
the Grant administration. The prospect of a national victory encouraged
several Democrats to seek the nomination, but standing above all the
potential candidates was New York Governor Samuel Tilden.

Although by 1876 the sixty-two-year-old Tilden had amassed a fortune and possessed an admirable political resume, he did not reach national prominence until 1874. It was in that most Democratic election
year, that Tilden, running as a reform candidate, captured the governor's
mansion in New York. Tilden's reputation as a reformer resulted from
his battles with William Marcy "Boss" Tweed. Tweed, the head of the
powerful political machine known as Tammany Hall, ran New York City

politics and along the way built an untold wealth from bribes and kick-backs. No one knows just how much money Tweed managed to plunder from New York, but most estimates put it between $75 million and $200 million in just a two-year period. Most notoriously, Tweed was behind the construction of the New York County Courthouse, a building that in 1862 cost almost $14 million, most of it going into his and party workers' hands. Working at the behest of the city comptroller, Tilden published a thorough analysis of Tweed's bank records, one that showed the complex schemes of kickbacks and payoffs that had netted him millions. Tweed never recovered from these revelations, and eventually he died in a jail just a few blocks from his birthplace. As governor, Tilden brought the same zeal to breaking up the infamous "Canal Ring"—a bipartisan group of public officials who, working through corrupt contractors, bilked the state out of millions of dollars for work on the state's inland canals.

A reformer was what the Democrats needed. As one historian noted, the platform put forth in St. Louis could be summarized in one word, reform.[2] "Reform" was not just about corruption, as the Democrats used it; every issue would be solved by reform. The economy would be restored, but only by reform. The currency difficulty could be solved by reform. Even the southern question—when and how to end reconstruction—called for reform. Not surprisingly, Tilden "the reformer" was the heavy favorite going into the convention. It took only two ballots for Tilden to lock down the nomination. The final tally had Tilden with 535 votes (72 percent) and Thomas Hendricks, still his closest rival, with just 60. At that point it was moved and approved that the nomination would go to Tilden unanimously. The evening's work done, the convention adjourned for the night having nominated for the third straight time a candidate from New York. But this time, the Democrats were convinced that they had a winner.

Results of the 1876 Election

PART I

As was still the custom in 1876, neither candidate publicly campaigned. They stayed behind the scenes in their respective gubernatorial posts. Of course, they maintained contact with their political operatives, although Tilden was rather more aloof from the campaign than was Hayes. Indeed, Tilden's reticence to take responsibility for directing his own campaign caused great consternation among Democratic leaders. At the start of the campaign, Republicans had been greatly worried that Tilden would use substantial portions of his vast fortune to finance the campaign. As it turned out, Tilden contributed little of his millions; to him, principle required that party members should shoulder party efforts. The Republicans, however, had a ready supply of contributions from federal employees. It was understood that the many patronage appointments in the federal service would contribute at least 2 percent of their salary to the party.

Tilden's diffidence was also apparent, as he procrastinated over his acceptance letter. According to the custom of the day, once nominated the candidates were to write letters accepting the nomination and outlining their views on the issues. Hayes completed his within about a month of the convention, and although it did not please everyone in his party, it was generally well received. Conversely, Tilden's was not completed until early August. Unfortunately for him, delay did not improve the quality of the letter. What Tilden ultimately produced was a lengthy document, of almost impenetrable prose, littered with arcane references and nuanced policy statements. It was a campaign essay that few voters could understand.

Acceptance letters aside, to no one's surprise the campaign played out largely through negative attacks, most of them launched by the Republicans. Republican strategy in 1876 was a replay of 1872. Hayes's spokesmen continually attacked Tilden because he was a Democrat. Voters were constantly reminded that it was the Republicans who saved the Union, when Democrats sought to tear it asunder. Former Union soldiers were encouraged to "vote the way you shot," and audiences across the country were reminded that "the man who assassinated Abraham Lincoln was a Democrat." By 1876, waving the "bloody shirt" was a well-practiced Republican strategy.

But there were also personal attacks on Tilden. Robert Ingersoll, speaking on Hayes's behalf and at his request, not so subtly implied that the never married Tilden was a homosexual. In case the voters missed the implications of Ingersoll's speeches, the most famous political cartoonist of the day, Thomas Nast, frequently drew Tilden in a dress. The most serious blow came from the Republican *New York Times* in which he was accused of underpaying his taxes during the Civil War. It turns out that there was no truth to the story, but it took Tilden almost a month to reply with the facts. His own inclination was to ignore the charges. The much delayed response came only because party leaders beseeched one of Tilden's close friends to ride herd on the candidate until he answered the charges. But Tilden refused to take the offensive and attack Hayes. He was given several grounds on which Hayes was vulnerable, including the fact that the Republican standard bearer had paid no income taxes in 1868 and 1869. Tilden simply refused to go on the attack.

As Election Day approached, Hayes and the Republicans began preparations for their defeat. Within the party leadership, no one thought that they were likely to win a majority of the Electoral College, although they did have scenarios under which Hayes could win. But even the rosiest projections depended on winning some unlikely states. Democratic party officials had very similar projected numbers.

On November 7, 1876, both Hayes and Tilden retired for the evening, confident of the results. Based on the vote counts they were receiving, they even agreed on the outcome. Hayes went to bed believing that he had lost and Tilden called it a night confident that he was to be the next president of the United States. Most of the nation's papers echoed this verdict. Even the solidly Republican *Chicago Tribune* headlined its November 8 edition, "Lost, The Country Given Over to Democratic Greed and Plunder."

Almost alone among the major newspapers, the *New York Times* held out, entitling an editorial in the November 8 edition, "A Doubtful Election." The *Times* then proceeded to suggest that Hayes would win if the Republicans took New Jersey and Florida. Later editions reflecting more up-to-date vote counts provided different scenarios under which Hayes would win. By midday on November 8, the parties had fairly complete numbers and largely agreed that Tilden had a total of 184 votes to Hayes's 166, with three states still unaccounted. It was also clear that even though Tilden needed one more electoral vote to gain the majority, he had received a majority of the popular vote.

Both parties assumed that the election would be decided by three southern states—Florida, South Carolina, and Louisiana—the three southern states not yet redeemed. Early reports had Tilden winning all three states, but the votes would need to be certified by the returning boards (certifying boards) in each of the three states. With the election in the balance, both parties sent delegations of highly experienced politicians to the states. The parties blanketed the states with representatives, sending investigators out across the states to take depositions substantiating charges of fraud or voter suppression. Suspecting the worst, the leaders of the delegations stayed in touch with party headquarters by the use of secret codes, lest their findings be prematurely revealed to the other party.

Florida. Of the three southern states, Florida was the closest. The first count had Tilden winning by ninety-one votes. The returning board was composed of three state officials—two Republicans and one Democrat, although the latter had been appointed the state's attorney general as a reward for supporting Grant in 1872. At the end of the first day, the board reported that Hayes led by forty-three votes. As it turned out, this was a mistake based on an account from one county where the election board had thrown out two Democratic precincts based on rumors that a few illegal votes had been cast. The returning board restored these votes, giving Tilden a ninety-four-vote lead. But by that time the whole world had heard that Hayes had carried Florida. Next on tap for the returning board was Alachua County. For two days the board deliberated charges by Democrats that the county's count contained votes cast after the polls closed. Despite the fact that two poll workers testified to being paid to ignore the illegal votes, the returning board found insufficient evidence to throw out the votes. The decision on the votes in Alachua County so upset one Republican observer, General Francis Barlow (founder of the American Bar Association), that he left Florida, with his reputation for integrity intact but his promising career in the Republican Party in tatters. On December 5, the day before the electors were to meet, the board announced its final results—Hayes had carried the state by 924 votes.

South Carolina. In South Carolina, the state with the most pre-election violence and the largest presence of federal troops, the first returns showed the state's seven electoral votes going to Hayes, but they also had the Democratic candidate for governor in the lead. The battle before the returning board in South Carolina was over the legislative elections. State law authorized the legislature to certify the winner of the gubernatorial election; the returning board should have certified all other elections. Democrats fearful that the all-Republican returning board would disqualify enough Democratic legislative candidates to deprive their candidate the governor's post, appealed to the state's supreme court. The Republican-dominated court ordered the returning board to simply endorse the given vote totals. But the board ignored the court ruling and disqualified votes from two Democratic counties. The court then ordered that the board provide an official vote total, but the returning board quickly adjourned to avoid the court's decision. Angered by the adjournment, the court ordered the board members arrested for contempt. A friendly Republican magistrate promptly released them.

Meanwhile, both parties claimed control of the legislature. After a one-day walkout, Democrats returned to the chambers and two separate legislatures proceeded to act as though they were the lawful governing body of South Carolina. On December 6, the Republican electors met and cast their votes for Hayes. These votes were certified and sent to Washington as the electoral votes of South Carolina. That same day, the Democrats' electors met and cast their votes for Tilden. In turn these votes were transmitted to Washington. The action of the Democrats was perplexing because they had not seriously contested Hayes's victory. Nevertheless, Congress was about to receive two slates of electoral candidates from the state.

Louisiana. In Louisiana, the Democrats seemingly amassed a substantial lead in the presidential election. Early returns had Tilden leading by more than six thousand votes. After numerous days of open sessions in which the board examined returns from several parishes, it went into secret session. On December 4, the all-Republican board announced that despite the early reports, Hayes had actually carried the state. Citing systematic intimidation of voters, the board disqualified a little over fifteen thousand votes, thirteen thousand of these votes having been for Tilden. The Hayes votes certified by the returning board were transmitted to Congress, but so too were the votes for Tilden. Democratic officials in Louisiana simply forwarded their state's eight electoral votes as cast for Tilden.

Oregon. As if the controversies surrounding the returning boards were not enough, there was also the problem of a disputed electoral vote in Oregon. One of the Republican electors was a postmaster, a job that clearly disqualified him for the post of elector. (The Constitution, Article II, Section 1, Clause 2, specifies that, "…no Senator or Representative, or Person holding an Office of Trust or Profit under the United States, shall be appointed an Elector.") In response to the disqualification of this elector, the Oregon governor, a Democrat, certified a replacement elector as the one receiving the fourth highest vote—a Democrat. The governor then transmitted the votes of three electors, two for Hayes and one Tilden. Republicans, for their part, also submitted a list of electoral votes, but their listing had all three votes for Hayes.

On December 6, the electors met in their respective states to cast their votes for president. In thirty-two states this was the usual pro forma affair. But in four states the electoral slates were in contention. Each of these four states—Florida, Louisiana, South Carolina, and Oregon— were sending Congress two slates with different counts.

PART II

As Congress reconvened in December it was obvious to all that a tidal wave of controversy was heading to Washington. Nothing less than the choice of the president was at stake. The winner would be determined by which of these disputed electoral slates Congress accepted. More fundamentally, the issue came down to who counted the votes. The Twelfth Amendment, ratified to avoid the problems encountered in the election of 1800, specifies that, "the President of the Senate shall, in the presence of the Senate and House of Representatives, open all certificates and the votes shall then be counted." But who is to do the counting? Republicans argued that the president of the Senate was charged with counting the votes as well as opening them—representatives were simply spectators. In this case, since there was no vice president, the task would fall to the Senate's acting president, Thomas W. Ferry, Republican senator from Michigan. Fearing that the acting president would simply ignore the votes for Tilden in the contested states, Democrats argued that the Speaker of the House of Representatives, a Democrat, should do the counting. Additionally, the parties disagreed over how the votes should be treated. Should the slates be accepted on their face, or should Congress investigate the validity of the votes? Republicans believed that the votes should be taken at face value, and the Democrats believed that Congress must investigate and make its own determinations.

After a month of increasingly heated deliberations, Congress agreed to refer the issue to a bipartisan commission. This commission was to be composed of five members from the House, five from the Senate, and five Supreme Court justices. The House was to select three Democrats and two Republicans. Conversely, the Senate was to be represented by three Republicans and two Democrats. As for the Justices, two were to be Democrats, two Republicans, and the fifth was expected to be an independent. All assumed the fifth Supreme Court Justice would have the power to break the inevitable ties that would result from the expected partisan voting. Furthermore, all participants assumed that the fifth justice would be David Davis, the only independent on the Court.

Hopes for a truly bipartisan commission quickly fell apart, however. On the same day that Congress passed the legislation, the Illinois legislature resolved its deadlock over the selection of a U.S. senator. Democrats and members of the small Greenback Party combined to select Justice Davis to fill the seat. Republicans quickly assumed that Davis had been named to the post in order to secure his vote on the commission. If true, the Democrats made a bad deal, because Davis promptly and definitively refused to serve on the commission.

Having committed to resolving the dispute by the creation of the commission, Democrats were in a difficult position. A fifth Justice would be a Republican, there being only two Democrats on the Court. But if they refused to accept another member, the deal would fall apart. In addition, they suspected that the acting president of the Senate would simply accept the disputed Republican votes. Eventually the Democrats accepted Justice Joseph P. Bradley, a President Grant appointee to the Court.

In order to give the commission time to do its work, Congress moved the day for opening the electoral votes up from February 14 to February 1. On that day, the acting president of the Senate began opening the votes and calling out the results. Anticipation was high as the roll call proceeded to Florida. Would the acting president honor the deal that had been made? When Florida's time came, objections to counting the votes were immediately entered, and the acting president of the Senate referred the votes to the commission and adjourned for the day. Now everything turned on the decisions of the Electoral Commission.

Taking up their charge on the following day, the commission members began by hearing arguments from both sides in the Florida case. On the fifth day, the commissioners by a straight party vote ruled that they would receive no more evidence regarding Florida and that the electoral votes from that state would go to Hayes. Then as the weeks passed, one-by-one the commission considered the remaining contested states. In each case the results were the same; on straight partisan lines, Hayes received the electoral votes. Every contested electoral vote went to Hayes. As each state was decided, the Senate approved the commission report, so that when all the contested elections were determined, the formal counting of the votes was a simple formality.

Still the process needed to be completed. For many hours the Congress engaged in fractious debate with threats of filibuster and members, some holding pistols, screaming "fraud!" Finally, at 4:30 a.m. on Saturday March 2, 1877, the acting president of the Senate declared the proceedings closed and Rutherford B. Hayes the victor. The final vote was Hayes 185, Tilden 184. Hayes by one electoral vote was declared the winner even though he had placed second in the popular vote. Even after losing thousands of votes at the hands of the returning boards, Tilden still commanded a majority of the popular vote. Two days later, Hayes was sworn in as president of the United States.

How Hayes Could Have Lost

For the Democrats, the 1876 election was a very painful loss. It was not simply that they had lost a close election under questionable circumstances; it was that they had lost an election that was clearly theirs to lose. They should have won it. Everything pointed to a victory for the Democrats. With a constant outpouring of scandals and economic depression gripping the nation, Democrats had entered the election year filled with hope.

Obviously, Tilden could have won the election if just one of the contested southern states had gone his way. Louisiana was a particularly hard loss for Democrats. The thirteen thousand Democratic votes thrown out in that state were clearly beyond anything they had expected. To

Democrats, this was the stolen election. In the rough and tumble world of nineteenth-century American elections, fraud, bribery, and voter suppression were common practices. Were these activities present in the contested states? Of course they were; that much is indisputable. It is also true that Republicans as well as Democrats engaged in these activities. Undoubtedly Democrats were more successful than Republicans in the contested southern states, but no one had clean hands. The problem is that with widespread corruption, lacking good measures, and under severe time pressures, the partisan nature of the decisions is hardly surprising.

Tilden Is Actively Involved

Clearly with the returning boards staffed by Republicans, the odds were against the Democrats. Nevertheless, Tilden watched them operate from the sidelines. Tilden's advisers warned him that he could lose the southern states, even Louisiana, but he refused to believe it. Over and over again, Tilden confidently clung to the belief that justice would prevail.

He was repeatedly exhorted to enter the fray with public statements calling on Americans around the country to rally to his side. Fearful that public assemblies would incite violence and convinced that principled Republicans would never tolerate fraud, Tilden stayed silent. Tilden's advisers were particularly wary of the Louisiana election. Republicans dominated the returning boards in Florida and South Carolina, but they were men of prominence and character. That was certainly not the case in Louisiana. There the board members were men of low repute, generally thought of by Republicans and Democrats alike as scoundrels. Still the presidential candidate remained silent. It was inconceivable to him that he could lose the election.

As it became apparent that the three southern states were going to be contested, party officials and friends urged Tilden to seek out Hayes. Most believed that Hayes would agree to a joint committee of "eminent citizens" to oversee the returns in the South. Although Tilden could not have known it at the time, Hayes may well have agreed. Hayes believed until the eleventh hour that he had lost the election. In fact, he may well have conceded a day or two after the vote were if not for the fact that party officials—backed by a *New York Times* series of articles—convinced him that he might have a chance. Again, Tilden did nothing.

A focus on the southern states missed other opportunities for a Tilden victory, however. After all, if the commission had accepted the Oregon governor's electoral slate—two Republicans and one Democrat—the final vote totals would have been reversed. The final count would have been Tilden 185 and Hayes 184. Even though it was well known that one of the Republican electors was a federal official and therefore ineligible to serve as an elector, the Democratic secretary of state in Oregon signed the certification papers for all three Republicans. This gave the commission the cover they needed, on a straight party vote they accepted the certification of the secretary of state and rejected that of the governor, even though this directly contradicted what they had done in Florida.

COLORADO IS NOT YET A STATE

Additionally, Colorado is often overlooked, but that state played a pivotal role in the election of Hayes. In 1876 the congressional Democrats had approved the long delayed statehood for Colorado. Republicans had delayed this decision reluctant to grant statehood because it would deprive them of valuable patronage positions—positions that would be filled by the state once it ceased to be part of a federal territory. Democrats, based on information supplied by a territorial representative, believed that were Colorado to be admitted into the Union it would vote Democratic. Colorado was admitted to the Union on August 1, 1876; nine weeks later elections for the state legislature and governor were held. Anticipating the short time between the state elections and the presidential election as well as the excessive cost of two elections, Congress authorized the state legislature to select the electors. Much to the surprise and chagrin of Democrats, voters in the new state elected a Republican governor and a Republican-controlled state legislature. They promptly appointed three electors pledged to Hayes.

Had the Democrats simply stalled on Colorado's admission, putting it off just one year, Tilden would have won the election, despite losses in the contested southern states. Tilden would have stood at 184 electoral votes, but Hayes would have been reduced to 182. Without Colorado's participation in the election, 184 votes would have constituted a majority.

TILDEN TOOK AN OATH

Finally, the day after the acting president of the Senate declared Hayes the winner, the House of Representatives passed a resolution declaring Tilden the winner. The resolution gave him 196 electoral votes (including Florida and Louisiana) and Hayes was awarded 173. Tilden was sent a congratulatory telegram and urged to take the oath of office. Of course Tilden, much to the disgust of many of his followers, declined, believing that the resolution lacked authority. To many of his supporters, his failure to act on the resolution demonstrated that he lacked courage. In truth, accepting the House resolution would have only inflamed the situation and may well have led to violence and rebellion. Tilden's greatest contribution may be that he demonstrated the truth of Shakespeare's adage, "The better part of valor is discretion."

If Hayes Had Not Been Elected

Given the heated contest the surprising thing about the election of 1876 is how little the candidates actually disagreed on the major issues of the day. This should not be too surprising as both parties selected moderate governors from northern states who were fiscal conservatives, interested in government reform, and committed to hard money (the view that currency must be backed by gold).

Had Tilden been elected he would have had two clear advantages over Hayes. First of all, as the winner of the popular vote, Tilden would not have been called an illegitimate president—a charge that dogged Hayes for years. Secondly, unlike Hayes, Tilden never promised to be a one-term president, thus making him a lame duck on his first day in office. Nevertheless, Tilden's moral high ground may well have eroded with the 1878 revelations of the so-called Cipher Telegrams. These messages implicated Tilden in a plot to bribe election officials in three contested states. A subsequent congressional investigation cleared Tilden of any personal involvement, but his spotless reputation was damaged.

THE END TO RECONSTRUCTION

As president, Hayes is best remembered for ending Reconstruction. Depending on one's vantage point, this ending could be seen as a restoration of legitimate state government or an outright betrayal of the rights of the recently emancipated slaves. One of the reasons that this remains his most memorable legacy is that it fits the historical suspicion that Hayes became president by cutting a deal with southerners. According to a legend, Hayes agreed to withdraw troops from the South to secure a promise by southern senators not to block his election by a filibuster. There is doubt as to whether such a deal was ever struck.

Long a staple of the folklore surrounding the election of 1876, the story exaggerates Hayes's options. It is true that as president, Hayes did withdraw the troops, but his predecessor, President Grant, had already begun the process, and it was clear that there was little northern support for the continued deployment of federal troops in the southern states. House Democrats had made it clear that this was their aim by withholding funds to support the troops. Moreover, there is little reason to believe that Tilden would have handled the issue differently, especially if he owed his election to the contested states. Most likely, the shameful abandonment of the recently emancipated slaves would have gone forward under either administration.

THE CURRENCY PROBLEM

Both Hayes and Tilden were advocates of hard money. Neither of them favored schemes to inflate the currency, even though this was popular among many, especially westerners. Most likely, Tilden as well as Hayes would have vetoed the Bland-Allison Act of 1878, which required the government to create millions of dollars based on silver.[3] Nevertheless, little noticed in Tilden's dense letter accepting his party's nomination a scheme to gradually redeem the currency for gold. Had he, as president, been successful at implementing his proposal, farmers and other debtors may have received at least partial relief from their crushing debt, but hard money would have continued to reign.

CIVIL SERVICE REFORM

Again, the candidates agreed on the need to reform government service. There is no doubt that Hayes was committed to reform. His nomination of noted reformer Carl Schurz to be secretary of the interior signaled his intent. Schurz, who had earned the ire of Radical Republicans in 1872 when he chaired the Liberal Republican's Convention that nominated Horace Greeley, prohibited the removal of employees at the Interior Department except for cause and put in place merit examinations for positions in that department. His efforts to remove patronage were generally met with loathing and were of limited success, but they did demonstrate Hayes's interest in civil service reform. More generally Hayes was never able to enact significant reform legislation. Here, Tilden may have been more successful. As the candidate of reform, he and his fellow Democrats would have been under some pressure to deliver on their promises. Since Tilden ran as a reformer, he would have been expected to deliver at least some reform efforts.

LABOR UNREST

Hayes's most enduring legacy is the ending of Reconstruction, but he is also remembered for ending the 1877 labor strikes afflicting the railroads. With the nation still suffering from the depression that began in 1873, railroads had for years steadily reduced the pay and increased work demands on their employees. Then in 1887 workers in West Virginia went on strike to protest their second wage cut that year. Soon the strike spread as far west as St. Louis and Chicago and along the way it turned violent. Initially, state militia dealt with the strikers, but as rail traffic slowed and several railroads teetered on the brink of bankruptcy, President Hayes sent federal troops to quell the strikes. Hayes justified his use of troops as necessary to guarantee mail delivery.

The irony of the president who pulled troops out of the South being the first president to use troops to end a domestic labor dispute was not lost on the workers. If anything it hardened the resolve of both workers and employers and set up the 1880s as the decade of severe labor strife. It is highly unlikely that Tilden would have used federal troops in this situation. Tilden was certainly closely tied to railroad interests, even more so than Hayes. But the workers were his party's constituency, and to attack his political supporters would have been political suicide. The Democratic Party would have been ripped apart.

Conclusion

One hundred years after the signing of the Declaration of Independence, the nation experienced a bitter contest that could have erupted into nationwide violence. A candidate for the presidency who could not command a plurality of the national vote won the office through extra-constitutional proceedings of dubious validity. All of this occurred in an election year that saw the highest voter turnout in American history: almost 81.6 percent of registered voters came to the polls that year.[4]

For most countries, this clearly confusing electoral situation is cause for a political coup or a major conflict. This wasn't the case for the United States. Bitterly divided as the nation was, it struggled through. Tilden, for his part, refused to inflame public opinion and Hayes was the gracious victor. Hayes completed his term and quelled much of the hostility that greeted his inauguration. Even though it was a bitter loss for Democrats, they continued to work within the political system, finally capturing the White House eight years later.

— 3 —

1916: WILSON DEFEATS HUGHES— NO WAR, NOT YET

1916: The Election Year

THE COUNTRY AND THE WORLD

Technology and science brought significant changes to the lives of millions of people in the early twentieth century. The general thinking of the growing middle and upper-middle class in Europe and North America was that the increasing prosperity was normal, and that the world had reached a long period of stability and growth. In the field of political ideas, progressivism gained significant strength. Supporters of progressivism were increasingly convinced that a responsible government and concerned citizens should engage in a deliberate and planned "intervention" in many areas of life. Today we commonly call such planned interventions "social policy" and consider it an essential part of government's responsibilities. One hundred years ago, this policy was, in fact, a radical innovation. Progressivism emphasized the role of moral values, social justice, science, and education.

Unfortunately, the atrocities of World War I crushed the optimistic ideas of social progressivism. The battles of the Great War—this is how the war was called then—started in 1914 and ending five years later—took more than nineteen million lives and left another twenty-one million wounded worldwide. The United States alone lost 116,000 people during the two years of America's involvement, twice the number of casualties in the Vietnam War sixty years later. People witnessed physical destruction of cities, an explosion of nationalism, and cruelty and irrationality of their fellow human beings. World War I had seriously undermined the progressive belief in the ability of human beings of achieving peace, self-management, and prosperity.

Results of the 1916 Presidential Election

Entering the 1916 election year, America remained a vigilant and nervous witness of the war. Confronted by their own problems at home, the American people were generally unwilling to get involved in the midst of a bloody faraway conflict. The Democrats wanted to retain their power in the White House and Congress. The GOP's ultimate prize was returning to power after their 1912 defeat. The Republican Party had won all presidential elections since the Civil War allowing only two Democratic presidents, Cleveland in 1892 and Wilson. However, back in 1912 the Republicans were deeply divided by the inner-party split and the emergence of the Progressive Party. The "Progressives" supported former President Theodore Roosevelt and the conservatives followed the incumbent President William Taft. As the result, Woodrow Wilson, a Democrat, won the presidency in 1912 by the majority of the electoral vote but with only 41.8 percent of the general vote competing against Taft and Roosevelt.

In 1916, the GOP appeared unified and overcoming the embarrassment of the previous election. The Republican Party nominated U.S. Supreme Court Justice Charles Evans Hughes as a presidential candidate. Hughes was a well-known national figure with rich experience in government, law, and business. He was governor of the State of New York for almost four years until 1910. In that year, President Taft appointed Hughes to the Supreme Court bench and the Senate unanimously voted to confirm him. He retained his seat until June 10, 1916, when he resigned to accept the Republican nomination for president. According to his own comments, he accepted his nomination reluctantly believing that a member of the Supreme Court was not supposed to seek a political office. His advisers persuaded him to reconsider.

Hughes appeared to be a solid candidate who could reunite the party by appealing to both its traditional conservative and more liberal, progressive wings. An honest, straightforward, and compassionate man, he seemed well prepared to deal with domestic issues as well as foreign matters. The Republican presidential convention was held in Chicago in June 1916. Hughes was nominated on the third ballot. Charles Fairbanks, former senator from Indiana and former vice president under Theodore Roosevelt, was nominated as a candidate for vice president.

What were Hughes's chances to win the election? Was he the right candidate? In today's terms, he was an underdog, yet a very strong one. Hughes led a seemingly unified Republican Party. Initial surveys of public opinion, which were conducted quite differently in those days compared to contemporary scientific opinion polls (they were face-to-face and not based on random sampling), showed that Hughes was doing well, especially in big cities. He appeared to be a candidate who could make the race competitive and who could return the Republicans to the White House. Supported by former President Taft, the party had adopted a competitive progressive agenda compatible with that of the incumbent president and the Democratic Party candidate Woodrow Wilson.

However, the circumstances were not necessarily favorable for the Republicans in that year. The Democratic Party was in good shape politically. The party controlled the White House for four years and managed to stay away from major political blunders or scandals. Local organizations were united behind President Wilson. The country's economy was working steadily with 40 percent of people in the labor force.[1] The country's population had reached a symbolic threshold of 100 million in 1915 and kept growing steadily. Despite the ongoing world war, America's policy of non-involvement was seemingly supported by a majority of American people. These were all favorable factors increasing Wilson's chances for reelection. As president, Wilson faced almost no opposition within the Democratic Party. He was nominated along with Vice President Thomas Marshall in June 1914.

In November, Wilson won in thirty states and defeated Hughes by approximately 600,000 votes. Yet in the Electoral College, his victory was extremely slim: 277 versus 254 votes. The difference was only 23 votes, which meant that had Hughes won just 12 additional electoral votes, he would have become president. California as a state would have provided the necessary 13 votes. The Republican nominee swept most states east of Minnesota and South Dakota. Wilson won decisively in the South and West. The electoral results were so close that at 8 a.m. on Wednesday, several newspaper editorials greeted Hughes as a sure president-elect. He refused to support these unconfirmed reports and waited. He didn't know that President Wilson already had a contingency plan in case he lost the election. Wilson would have appointed Charles Hughes as secretary of state. Then he would have resigned the presidency immediately. Secretary of State Lansing and Vice President Marshall would have resigned, too. According to the law, in this case, the secretary of state would become president. Of course, Hughes could have refused to agree with this plan and might have waited until the official date of his inauguration.

In reality, with more states reporting the official returns, the electoral situation was becoming gloomy for Hughes. By Thursday, Wilson was ahead 257 against 251 without California, Minnesota, North Dakota, and New Mexico. It wasn't until Friday morning that the Wilson presidency was finally confirmed.

Wilson: How He Could Have Lost the 1916 Election

Hughes Stands Out

When two candidates run on relatively similar political platforms, it is crucial for the challenger to distinguish himself before the electorate. Similar to advertising, you must persuade consumers why they have to switch from one brand to another. In many ways, Wilson and Hughes were similar as individuals and presidential candidates. They both were children of clergymen, were university professors, served as governors of neighboring states, and shared many comparable progressive ideas about an active role of government in people's lives. Both wanted to see America strong and protected in a new and dangerous world. They both had a vision of America as a world leader. Although Hughes was six years younger than Wilson, age never became an issue during the electoral campaign. Both candidates wanted to appear as mature men and seasoned public officials.

What, then, could Hughes do to distinguish himself during the campaign? In 1916, the main source of information about political candidates was the newspapers and, to some degree, radio. Although Hughes was governor of New York, he did not have significant media exposure outside the state compared to today's governors of large states. Although Hughes had an attractive, progressive domestic agenda, Wilson had more media visibility as president. Moreover, his massive institutional reforms were widely known, including the creation of the Federal Reserve System in 1913, the Federal Trade Commission in 1914, and the Federal Farm Loan Act of 1916. One of the substantial advantages for Wilson was his image of a true patriot of the nation with a peace plan to keep America out of the devastating European war.[2] Hughes, in contrast, was a reliable and mature candidate but still not known well enough by the masses to swing the votes of the undecided or attract first-time voters. He believed his public service record would speak for itself. However, it was not enough. Hughes probably needed the Wilson administration to commit a profound mistake, a mistake serious enough to help Hughes distinguish himself as an alternative to Wilson. Hughes could have taken advantage of a serious, existing crisis.

EXAGGERATE THE DANGERS OF THE WAR

For campaign purposes, to increase his national exposure Hughes could have stressed and exaggerated the threat that America was facing from Germany. He could have used the facts about German submarine attacks against commercial and civilian vessels and Berlin's secret plans to invade Great Britain as evidence of the grave threat. He also could have appealed to America's nationalism by depicting Wilson as just a "soft" administrator, not a true commander-in-chief. Hughes could have launched a consistent and sharp criticism of Wilson's defense policies. Furthermore, he could have sparked a national debate using the existing disagreements within Washington's competing factions about the U.S.

role in the growing world conflict. Some experts supported decisive actions against Germany in defense of Great Britain while others believed that America could and should stay neutral.

Nevertheless, Hughes faced within the country very serious opposition to the war. Some opposed the war for nationalistic or ethnic reasons: the vast majority of Americans had their immediate relatives in Europe and particularly in the feuding countries, such as France, Germany, Austria, Russia, and England. Others maintained an old, traditional type of isolationist views following the advice of George Washington not to get into "entanglements" abroad and to avoid "infecting" the young democracy with militarism and imperialism practiced by European powers. Others opposed the involvement in the conflict for ideological reasons. On the left, socialists and communists accused the fighting nations of conducting the war to generate profit for the ruling classes and big corporations. On the right, a significant number of nationalists believed that it was not in the best interest of America to participate in any war in Europe. Many industrialists also believed that an escalation of the war would harm international trade and commerce and would cripple industries for years to come. Hughes was aware of these views. Being a pragmatic person, he did not want to make any ideological commitments related to U.S. foreign policy before being elected president. Therefore, he was too cautious to make any specific predictions or announce plans.[3] These tactics disappointed some of his actual and potential supporters who believed that the United States should have a stronger military.

The Wilson campaign was focusing on America's neutrality using the slogan, "but we didn't go to war." His government, as he rightly claimed, did not fire a shot, did not orphan any child, and did not widow any wife. Wilson knew that the war was almost inevitable but continued to bring into play peaceful slogans for campaign purposes. Hughes, however, did not want to use scare tactics and exaggerate the war threats in order to attract additional votes, something that twenty-first-century candidates would do without hesitation in order to win.

1916 Presidential Election
State-by-State Popular and Electoral College Vote

State	Charles E. Hughes (Republican, NY)			Woodrow Wilson (Democrat, NJ)		
	Vote	%	ECV	Vote	%	ECV
ALABAMA	28,662	22	-	99,116	76	11
ARIZONA	20,522	35.4	-	33,170	57.2	3
ARKANSAS	48,879	28.7	-	112,211	66	9
CALIFORNIA	462,516	46.3	-	465,936	46.6	13
COLORADO	101,388	34.7	-	177,496	60.8	6
CONNECTICUT	106,514	49.8	7	99,786	46.7	-
DELAWARE	26,011	50.2	3	24,753	47.8	-
FLORIDA	14,611	18.1	-	55,984	69.3	6
GEORGIA	11,294	7	-	127,754	79.5	14
IDAHO	55,368	41.1	-	70,054	52.2	4
ILLINOIS	1,152,549	52.6	29	950,229	43.3	-
INDIANA	341,005	47.4	15	334,063	46.5	-
IOWA	280,439	54.3	13	221,699	42.9	-
KANSAS	277,658	44.1	-	314,588	50	10
KENTUCKY	241,854	46.5	-	269,990	51.9	13
LOUISIANA	6,466	7	-	79,875	85.9	10
MAINE	69,508	51	6	64,033	47	-
MARYLAND	117,347	44.8	-	138,359	52.8	8
MASSACHUSETTS	268,784	50.5	18	247,885	46.6	-
MICHIGAN	337,952	52.2	15	283,993	43.9	-
MINNESOTA	179,544	46.4	12	179,155	46.3	-
MISSISSIPPI	4,253	4.9	-	80,422	93.3	10
MISSOURI	369,339	46.9	-	398,032	50.6	18
MONTANA	66,933	37.6	-	101,104	56.8	4
NEBRASKA	117,771	41	-	158,827	55.3	8
NEVADA	12,127	36.4	-	17,776	53.4	3
NEW HAMPSHIRE	43,725	49.1	-	43,781	49.1	4
NEW JERSEY	268,982	54.4	14	211,018	42.7	-
NEW MEXICO	31,097	46.5	-	33,693	50.4	3
NEW YORK	879,238	57.5	45	759,426	44.5	-
N. CAROLINA	120,890	41.7	-	168,383	58.1	12
N. DAKOTA	53,471	46.3	-	55,206	47.8	5
OHIO	514,753	44.2	-	604,161	51.9	24
OKLAHOMA	97,233	33.3	-	148,123	50.7	10
OREGON	126,813	48.5	5	120,087	45.9	-
PENNSYLVANIA	703,823	54.3	38	521,784	40.2	-
RHODE ISLAND	44,858	51.1	5	40,394	46	-
S. CAROLINA	1,550	2.4	-	61,845	96.7	9
S. DAKOTA	64,217	49.8	5	59,191	45.9	-
TENNESSEE	116,223	42.7	-	153,280	56.3	12
TEXAS	64,999	17.4	-	287,415	77	20
UTAH	54,137	37.8	-	84,145	58.8	4
VERMONT	40,250	62.4	4	22,708	35.2	-
VIRGINIA	48,384	31.8	-	101,840	67	12
WASHINGTON	167,208	43.9	-	183,388	48.1	7
WEST VIRGINIA	143,124	49.4	7	140,403	48.5	1
WISCONSIN	220,822	49.4	13	191,363	42.8	-
WYOMING	21,698	41.8	-	28,376	54.7	3
	8,546,789	46.1	254	9,126,300	49.2	277

HUGHES WOOS THE PROGRESSIVES

A unified and strong party is a decisive factor influencing the electability of any party's candidate in every election. The Republicans overcame the 1912 crisis, when the party was effectively split into two factions, but were not unified enough to campaign on the same platform. A few important agreements were reached. The Republican presidential convention in June 1916 called for the party's unity. The platform adopted during the convention also reflected many progressive ideas. With the nation possibly facing war, the platform called for a stronger national defense, and for better economic and military preparedness.

However, Hughes failed to rise to the challenge to promote the progressive agenda to entice more supporters. One of the reasons was his opposition to some progressive policies, such as the federal government's involvement in business regulations. Hughes did not want to win by using political maneuvering. He preferred to win the electoral race on principles. For example, he seriously criticized the Adamson Act, a federal law passed by the Wilson administration to mandate an eight-hour day for railroad workers. First, he did not believe that the federal government should force such regulations on private business. Second, he claimed that this law was purely political and designed to get additional votes for Wilson. Hughes believed that arbitration was the correct way to resolve most labor disputes. Hughes also opposed the Sixteenth Amendment, ratified in 1913, which gave Congress "power to lay and collect taxes on incomes." Because the income tax at that time primarily affected people with relatively high income, the idea of "taxing the rich" was supported by many Progressives within the Republican Party, including farmers and industrial workers from the midwestern and western states. Many of them, as well as scores of Republican supporters of progressive policies who were unimpressed by Hughes's conservative views, deserted the Republican Party in November and voted for Wilson. Hughes wanted to have a unified party supporting him, but he did not want to change his political convictions for that purpose. If he achieved that goal by giving in to the Progressives' wishes, he would have become president.

Hughes Does Not Make a Tactical Mistake in California

The infamous California "incident" would have remained an obscure event in the history of political campaigns had it not affected the election of 1916 so profoundly. Hughes lost California by a razor-thin margin. Ambitions and emotions took over several top Republican leaders who were stubborn enough not to see the dire consequences of their politicking. Settling of old political scores was at the core of this history-defining moment. If Hughes had controlled the situation better, he would have lived in the White House.

California Governor Hiram Johnson, one of the founders of the Progressive Party, was campaigning for the nomination for the U.S. Senate and seeking support from both the traditional and progressive wings of the Republican Party. He was very popular in California, and the local party organizations appeared to be decisively behind him. It was only natural to assume that Johnson and Hughes could have helped each other as political candidates from the same party. Moreover, in the summer of that year, Governor Johnson personally told Hughes about his support of him. They did not have any personal reason to dislike each other. Yet the political forces behind both candidates did everything possible to compromise the acceptable arrangements for Hughes's visit to California. Advisers on both sides continued to discourage Hughes and Johnson from making mutual endorsements. Why?

With the weakening of the progressive movement, some prominent members of "the old guard" of the Republican Party wanted to weaken or even eliminate Johnson from the political field and further diminish the importance of the progressive movement. To some, this task was as much personal as it was political. Governor Johnson was Theodore Roosevelt's presidential running mate on the Progressive Party's ticket. Not only did the party lose the election, but the loss also derailed the incumbent Republican President Taft's attempt at a second term in 1912. Johnson was widely accused of giving away the White House to the Democrats. Therefore, some Hughes top advisers with a long memory did everything possible to keep him away from Johnson while the presidential candidate was visiting California. Many Republicans did not want

Hughes to associate himself closely with Johnson. Republican voters across the country would have probably perceived an open endorsement of Johnson negatively. The conservatives within the party warned Hughes not to support Johnson. They argued that he might get votes in California but lose big in other states. However, Hughes was under similar pressure to come out in support of Johnson. Many progressive followers openly suggested—and Hughes was aware of these threats—that they would vote for Democrat Wilson if Hughes did not openly endorse Johnson and his political platform in California. Overall, Hughes faced the prospect of losing California on Election Day.

The choice, then, that Hughes apparently faced was to either win California but lose in some other states, or to lose California but secure victories elsewhere. It was a tough situation that required serious political maneuvering, which Hughes did not want to do. His personality played a crucial role here. He had in the past frequently displayed an obsessive rigidity to adhere to some principles and not deviate from them. In California, he should have played politics by courting Johnson in some limited way. He did not. He wanted to win on his ideological principles and did not want to attract votes in California by simply supporting Johnson and the progressive wing. Hughes was caught in the crossfire of the hostile forces busy destroying each other. As a result, they failed to deliver a big win to the Republican Party.

One small event, however, could have changed the course of history. Despite the lack of formal preparations, Hughes wanted to visit California before August and make as many speeches as possible in an attempt to consolidate support on the West Coast. In August, both Hughes and Johnson were apparently at the same place, a few yards apart, at the Virginia Hotel in Long Beach. Hughes was not aware of this fact. A huge crowd of approximately five thousand people came there to greet him, and he spent all his time with the crowd talking and shaking hands. He did not even find the time to sit down for a meal. A few hours later, after he had left the hotel, he was told that, apparently unknown to his close advisers, Johnson was in the same hotel. For some reason, both groups did not meet. Johnson's people also said nothing to the governor about

Hughes being nearby. Both candidates expressed formal regrets about this mishap. If Hughes and Johnson had met even briefly, this impromptu meeting could have had a symbolically positive meaning. Hughes did not have to make formal announcements about him meeting with the governor. Johnson, though, could have claimed the support of the Republican presidential candidate. The fact that both candidates did not meet and greet each other was used by the adversaries on both sides to exaggerate the divisions between Hughes and Johnson.

Hughes lost California and its thirteen electoral votes by a slim margin. Johnson, however, won decisively by the margin of almost 300,000 votes. In the traditional strongholds of the progressive wing in northern California, Hughes did especially poor compared to his performance in the southern part of the state. Johnson certainly played a role in the Republicans' defeat in the presidential election. He lacked both the desire and political will to campaign for Hughes in California. It was a very close election, yet Hughes could have won with just some extra support of the Progressives. Although Socialist and Prohibition party candidates gathered more than 70,000 votes in November, there were scores of Johnson supporters who, had they voted for Hughes, could have decided the election. If California had voted for Hughes (he needed just 3,421 additional votes), he would have won the White House in 1916.

The hotel "mishap" was an example of both political ineptness and bad luck. Campaigning in that state, Hughes placed himself in the hands of many people who pursued their personal goals and apparently were more interested in defeating Governor Johnson than in electing Hughes.[4]

HUGHES AVOIDED SMALL TACTICAL MISTAKES

His six years on the Supreme Court had somewhat insulated Hughes from the daily political rough-and-tumble. As a result, his inexperience in campaigning led to several tactical mistakes. One of them was the appointment of William Wilcox as his campaign manager. Wilcox was a loyal supporter and former head of the Public Service Commission in New York City. To promote himself better as a candidate, Hughes needed a well-known political figure as a manager to provide important strategic advice. Hughes was aware of this necessity, but despite several mistakes by Wilcox, Hughes stuck with him.

Hughes lost by tiny margins in New Mexico (a little more than two thousand votes), North Dakota (less than two thousand votes), and New Hampshire (just six votes), and his campaign was under criticism for not doing enough in these states did get a few additional votes. Hughes could have spent more time across the Midwest, as he did in Michigan, the state he won along with a majority of midwestern states. Instead, his campaign spent too much time in the western states that, probably with the exception of California, were not likely to give him electoral votes. One of the reasons was the overwhelming opposition to war that was particularly strong in the western states, and based on that opposition, Hughes appeared "hawkish" to many uncommitted voters. In addition, Hughes might have generated better press coverage on the East Coast while campaigning around the country. Although he had several stenographers by his side so that his speeches in small towns in the West were immediately provided to local papers, that coverage did not get wide distribution. In addition, his campaign in the West went almost unnoticed by the big East Coast newspapers.

The strategy to get more women's votes in the West probably was not successful either. Although Hughes supported universal women's suffrage, he did not articulate this well enough to attract more women votes, particularly in the West. The Hughes campaign even sent a special promotional train to encourage female votes for Hughes. The train was sponsored by several wealthy families from the East Coast and did not have the mobilizing effect out West that the organizers had hoped for. Critics even suggested that the effort appeared a bit condescending; specifically, the perception was that women from the East Coast, in which many states did not have women's voting rights, attempted to encourage and instruct other women how to vote.

In today's terms, to win, Hughes should have acted as a politician building coalitions, promising immediate benefits to different groups, and appealing to people's emotions. However, Hughes was a man of principles first. His political decisions were rooted in his moral values. He wanted to be a man of virtue who stood above politics and intrigues. In close elections, a candidate's personality matters.

What If Wilson Were Not Elected?

After a narrow defeat, Hughes remained a concerned observer of a radical change in Woodrow Wilson's war policies following the 1916 election. He witnessed the Democratic Party rallying around the president. He felt an outburst of national support of the war effort. Hughes could only guess if the Democrats would have supported him as strongly if he, not Wilson, were elected president. He believed that it would not be the case and that furious political battles would have ensued between him and the Congress. Privately, Hughes mentioned that he was relieved about his loss in the election. He thought it was better to preserve national unity in the face of war, and that could be easier done if the same party were in the White House and in control of Congress.

Yet if he were elected in 1916, Hughes might have used the electoral results as a mandate to move America to accept a more active role in international affairs.

THE UNITED STATES JOINS THE LEAGUE OF NATIONS

Long before the war was over, some world leaders already began to think about a new international system that would no longer allow war. One idea was gaining strong support: an international organization of sovereign states. Hughes as a candidate supported this idea in 1916 as well as another initiative about a post-war international court comprised of full-time judges to deal with a wide range of issues including trade and border disputes.

In February 1919, the world leaders came to a peace conference in Paris to work on an international agreement (the Treaty of Versailles) to end the war and establish a new world order to keep a long-lasting peace. After several weeks of debates, a preliminary version of the agreement to establish a new international organization, the League of Nations, was released to the press. The text of the agreement appeared satisfactory to many observers back in the United States. The weakest link, however, was Article X, which proposed America's commitment "to respect and preserve as against external aggression the territorial integrity and existing political independence of all members of the league."

Article X was a seemingly general statement of support for the League, no more. Yet the acceptance of this Article would have meant a serious challenge to the U.S. Constitution. The acceptance would have meant that international circumstances—and not the U.S. Congress—would have automatically forced America into a war under the conditions of the treaty. In addition, the treaty proposed certain regulations on immigration and trade policies. The Republicans, who had won control of Congress in the 1918 elections and had enough power to block the ratification of the treaty, were ready for a political battle on Capitol Hill. Wilson accepted the challenge. His supporters maintained that in promoting the treaty the president acted on behalf of the nation and world peace. He was an idealist who believed that his country had to play a special role in the world. He believed that our civilization could not survive materially unless it were redeemed spiritually.[5] Wilson opponents portrayed him as a partisan warrior, stubborn and inflexible. In the end, Wilson lost the battle in the Senate and the United States never joined the League of Nations.

One of Wilson's mistakes was his inflexibility with regard to the treaty. He appeared too rigid and partisan. To make things worse, Wilson had very poor relations with Republican Senator Henry C. Lodge, chairman of the Foreign Relations Committee and a leading Wilson critic. The president did not want the Republicans to make changes to the document that he cherished in his heart.[6] Wilson tried to use various political and legal maneuvers to defeat the Republicans instead of seeking a reasonable compromise in the Senate. The Senate would have eventually adopted the agreement if the president did not instruct the Democratic senators to vote against the proposed amendments. Finally, in a period of twenty-two days, Wilson traveled more than eight thousand miles delivering thirty-seven long speeches. He wanted to bring the discussion about the treaty directly to the people. However, his serious illness (he suffered a stroke while on tour in Colorado) did not allow him to continue his battle.

Wilson's personality played an important role in his political defeat. One distinguishing feature of his character was his intolerance to opposition. This behavioral trait was evident during his presidency at Princeton University as well as during his New Jersey governorship. While personal convictions result in stubbornness, that might become a virtue in favorable political circumstances. Such circumstances were not favorable in Wilson's case.[7] During his second term in the White House, his compulsive authoritarianism became his serious political liability. He was impatient and did not like compromises, especially with the people he disliked.

Perhaps his inflexibility resulted from his fast ascendance to power. He rapidly moved from the presidency of Princeton into the complicated currents of New Jersey politics. In 1913, two years after he was elected governor, he became U.S. president as a result of favorable circumstances and the weakened Republican Party. When the Republicans gained control of Congress following the 1918 election, Wilson showed the lack of political flexibility and willingness to compromise. Key Democrats also believed that the Republicans wanted to derail the treaty at any cost in order to prevent the Democratic Party from entering the 1920 elections with a political advantage as the "party of peace." It was a reasonable position. Wilson's opponents believed that if he were successful in pushing the United States into the League of Nations—a world league to keep the peace—his party would be in power for many years.[8]

Would Hughes have acted differently as president? From the start of treaty negotiations, Hughes believed that Article X was a mistake. His position was that America should never accept an international institution as the authority over its foreign policy. Acknowledging the importance of U.S. participation in the League of Nations, Hughes suggested specific amendments that would have made the treaty acceptable. The amendments included the right of each member-nation to withdraw from the League on two years' notice. Second, the questions of immigration and tariffs would remain exclusively matters of individual states. Third, the United States would have no obligation to discuss with the League matters of concern related to U.S. foreign policy. Finally, and most importantly, only the U.S. Congress could determine whether the United States had an obligation to act according to Article X. Hughes had also advocated America's entry into the Permanent Court of International Justice (the World Court), which was authorized by the treaty.

These were quite reasonable amendments and would have been satisfactory to most U.S. senators. Hughes as president would have dealt with a friendly Senate, and a favorable political climate to push for America's membership in the League of Nations. Newspaper reporters, journalists, scholars, and many prominent politicians wanted a more substantial American integration in global policies. The challenge was to accept the country's integration on its own terms. Most European leaders, including those of Britain and France, could have approved the Senate's version of the treaty even with the suggested amendments. After ratification, it would have been the Republicans' turn to portray themselves as a party of peace and almost guarantee Hughes's reelection in 1920.

A DIFFERENT FOREIGN POLICY

Hughes had several charismatic features rooted in his honesty, integrity, and sense of responsibility. America was entering a long historic period of political adolescence, associated with the nation's growing strength but a diminished sense of restraint. Like Wilson, Hughes held that international society would do well to abide by the law to the highest extent possible, and that international institutions could play a constructive role in ensuring peace, progress, and prosperity. However, Hughes was not an idealist like Wilson. Hughes was a political leader using the principles of progressivism and international realism. He recognized the irreplaceable role of power sharing in international relations and believed that peace is not guaranteed by good intentions alone.

In international affairs, Hughes would have been more of a judge than an idealist. Hughes was a cautious and pragmatic leader, and a supporter of a new world order through adjudication—a legal mechanism and political tradition of promoting the global rule of law. He rejected "ethnic" loyalties in foreign policy. His 1916 campaign slogan was, "America first and America efficient." It was a call for national unity in dealing with domestic and international challenges. Hughes hoped that American foreign policy would not embrace a mixture of German-American, Irish-American, or other "hyphenated" interests. Putting America first was about America's unity as a nation: the United States should come first, not the interests of people's ancestral homelands.

Of course, constant challenges and conflicts would have required Hughes's unwavering attention. Mistakes and misfortunes would have been unavoidable. Relations with Mexico would have remained difficult regardless of the person in the White House. Hughes would certainly have opposed the new communist regime in Russia and could have easily antagonized the relations between the two countries. In the end, regardless of who was president, Mussolini could have risen to power in Italy and Hitler would have carried his plans to create a radical nationalist party. Japan's aggression in Manchuria in 1931, Italy's aggression against Ethiopia in 1935, and the Spanish Civil War in 1936 would have taken place.

However, if the United States had joined the League of Nations, this could have changed history. The League of Nations would have not hesitated to enforce peace, the task very much supported by Republican leaders, including Theodore Roosevelt, William H. Taft, and Henry Lodge. Belligerent states would have known that the League was strong enough to restrain them, and this could have significantly altered history. America's global domination in international relations would have started in the early 1920s.

EARLY DEVELOPMENT OF REALISM

To take a first step toward a new world order, America as a nation would need to be strong. Hughes would have pushed for significant military spending to provide for the nation's preparedness. He frequently criticized Wilson during the 1916 election campaign for the lack of such preparedness. He believed that military strength would have brought the United States security as well as respect around the world. Weakness, in his mind, brought insult and war.

Hughes was in a great position to implement the principles of realism—an approach to international relations based on power sharing and balancing state interests. For example, Hughes, as U.S. secretary of state appointed by President Harding, was an active promoter of the 1921–1922 Washington Conference. The goal of the conference was to balance the power of several nations in the Pacific. This conference and subsequent treaty put the brakes on an arms race that could have quickly led to a war in the 1920s.

PAYING FOR WAR

In April 1917, the United States declared war against Germany. An overwhelming majority of senators and representatives approved the declaration of war submitted to them by President Wilson. America turned to conscription. By the end of the war, more than 7 million people served in the military in various capacities. The total cost of the war was $33 billion. Where did the money come from? Mostly, the funds were provided through higher taxes and government bonds.

Historically, liberal governments compared to conservative ones do a more efficient job in times of war by raising taxes to pay for their country's military operations. Because the conservative governments are generally reluctant to raise taxes, this creates potential problems for them. Wilson did what was necessary from his point of view. He raised taxes. The U.S. Revenue Act of 1916 raised the lowest income tax rate from 1 to 2 percent on income up to $20,000, and raised the top rate to 15 percent on taxpayers with incomes above $2 million. A progressive tax system was established for incomes between these brackets. (Previously, the top rate had been 7 percent on income above $500,000.) The 1917 act further lowered the taxable income to $2,000 and the top bracket was raised to 67 percent of income. The heaviest responsibility of paying taxes was shifted to the wealthiest individuals and corporations.

Most probably, Hughes would have resisted such a radical tax increase and would probably have turned to tax incentives to businesses and corporations in order to increase production. He also could have turned to loans. President Wilson, in fact, using federal loans and borrowing, increased the federal debt twenty times since 1915, reaching $20 billion by 1920.[9] By the end of 1918, the cost of living had risen more than 70 percent. In that year, the Democratic Party suffered a defeat in the midterm elections. The Republicans gained control of the Congress.

Despite Wilson's high taxation, economic production boomed. Corporate profits also went up partially because of special laws guaranteeing profits on war-related work and a temporary suspension of antitrust laws. Hughes, although he could have pursued different tax and budgetary policies, would likely have achieved the same results. Most probably, Hughes could not have controlled the high retail prices and increasing inflation that occurred under Wilson.

XENOPHOBIA

During the war, what began as an atmosphere of national patriotism and enthusiasm was spoiled by a xenophobic rise in fear, suspicion, and intolerance. Hughes, of course, could have had only limited power to influence people's attitudes during the war. He could have done little to reverse the growth of anti-German sentiment. German music, books, songs, poetry, journals, and consumer products had disappeared from the radio programs, newspapers, and store shelves. Many schools stopped teaching German language and literature. People began to change the names of food products containing German ethnic or other words. Hamburgers were commonly labeled "liberty sandwiches" and "liberty cabbage" had replaced sauerkraut. This was a societal sentiment, a mixture of obsessive anxiety and fear. In many countries during a period of conflict with other states, similar renaming is commonplace. American coffee, French fries, and Russian vodka have similarly been targeted.

In addition to anti-German sentiment, Hughes could have also witnessed the rise of anti-communism in America. American public opinion had turned against anyone in the United States suspected of sympathizing with Russian bolshevism. Government raids, searches, warrantless arrests, and deportations became commonplace. The most vulnerable category was recent immigrants who did not receive a permanent status. Many of them were deported just for their alleged but unconfirmed affiliations with communist or radical organizations. Hughes could have probably done little to curtail the activities of the American Protective League, a private organization of approximately one quarter of a million people. The government, in fact, endorsed this group's activities directed against anyone who was against the war or expressed anti-American sentiment. The Espionage Act of 1917 and the Sedition Act of 1918 provided legal power to restrict activities of dissidents or anyone who simply disagreed with the government. Any antiwar action or antiwar information spread through the mail that would have caused any harm to the U.S. government and its war effort was punishable by law.

Neither Wilson nor Hughes could have stopped the mounting "witch-hunt" within the country each man's support for individual liberties. We have to understand their actions in the context of the situation in the nation. The United States was involved in a war. It came to almost every American home. Foreign threats were real. Hughes, like Wilson, would have supported the idea that to save America's freedom, some temporary measures to limit freedom were necessary. Both of them also believed that during war, people ought to subordinate their private interest to the general political purpose so that the country could prevail.

A DIFFERENT IMMIGRATION ACT OF 1924

A new immigration bill was prepared by 1924. The bill, supported by many political groups, was supposed to limit immigration to the United States. Frightened by the influx of newcomers from overseas, the American middle class was generally in favor of drastic steps to limit or curtail immigration. Labor unions also supported restrictions on immigration to protect jobs in manufacturing and agriculture. Congressional representatives from the Pacific Coast states demanded serious limitations on immigration, particularly from Japan and parts of Southeast Asia. Some nationalist groups demanded the preservation of ethnic and racial "purity" of the American nation. The most serious target of the bill were Japanese immigrants. Although immigration from Japan had been limited since the beginning of the twentieth century by the Gentlemen's Agreement, according to which the Japanese government stopped issuing foreign passports to most of its citizens willing to emigrate to the

United States, the new bill included a special provision known as an "exclusion act," which established even more serious limitations on Japanese immigrants (limiting immigration to about two hundred people per year).

Assuming that Hughes remained in the White House beyond 1920, he would have likely signed a different immigration act. There was a real possibility that Hughes would have had a chance and willingness to make important changes to the text of the bill, which could have positively affected U.S.-Japanese relations. Hughes was against the exclusion section of the bill. As secretary of state, he urged the Congress to eliminate the exclusion provision. He actually made several statements expressing his concern about the negative impact of the proposed legislation on U.S.-Japanese relations, which were improving after 1918. Japanese politicians and citizens alike considered the new immigration policy and the exclusion act as a national insult. For the Japanese people, to be excluded from migration was extremely shameful. The Japanese government understood that the United States had the right to close its borders, and that Japan had no presumed right to send its nationals to the United States. Yet the exclusion was a blow to Japanese pride that subsequently affected Japan's policies toward the United States. A loss of respect is often a loss of goodwill.

The House passed the bill including the exclusion provision, by a vote of 323 to 71. President Coolidge, after asking Congress to postpone implementation of the bill, reluctantly signed it into law. If he vetoed the bill, then the Congress had enough votes to override the veto. As Hughes had predicted, the inclusion of the discriminatory, anti-Japanese clause severely damaged Japanese-American relations, which Hughes had continuously cultivated for several years. The reaction in Japan was overwhelming. The immigration law with the exclusion provision was widely considered as an act of hostility from America. There were mass demonstrations in Japanese cities and calls for retaliation. Hughes tendered his resignation as secretary of state to President Coolidge. It was rejected.

As president, Hughes would have worked with the Congress to block passage of the anti-Japanese provision. He understood too well the importance of strategic relations with other nations, and Japan in particular. His persistence could have changed the political situation in Japan to some degree. The nationalists and militarists in Japan would have had fewer inflammatory arguments to use in their speeches and electoral campaigns in the 1920s. Japanese-American diplomatic and trade relations would have developed at least for a time, which would have affected the U.S. interpretation of Japanese aggressive policies in Asia in the 1930s. This could have postponed Washington's harsh responses to Japanese actions, and Japan would not have had plans to attack the United States immediately. There would have been no Pearl Harbor.

PROHIBITION REMAINS INTACT

Under President Wilson, Congress passed the Eighteenth Amendment in 1917. The so-called prohibition amendment banned the manufacture, transport, and sale of intoxicating liquors. The amendment, ratified on the state level, went into effect in 1920. For many years prior to the passage of the amendment, numerous social and religious groups pushed for tough measures against alcohol. In the 1916 presidential election, both candidates, Wilson and Hughes, almost ignored the sensitive prohibition issue, as was the case with both parties' political platforms. Both Democrats and Republicans had strong supporters and opponents of restrictions on alcohol ("wet" and "dry" factions), and the election was expected to be close, with neither candidate wanting to alienate any part of his political base.

Would Hughes, as president, have conducted a different anti-alcohol policy? There are accounts of his negative views about the Eighteenth Amendment. The *New York Times* on February 17, 1919, reported that Hughes was considering leading the states' legal battle against prohibition. He also argued that matters of local concern, which included prohibition, should be settled by individual communities free of the opinions of outsiders. He also spoke openly and critically about the amendment based on certain constitutional issues.[10] Hughes thought that legal restrictions would be unwise and impractical. However, and most importantly, Hughes also deeply believed in the people's right to amend the Constitution. Therefore, he would not have fought against the Eighteenth Amendment.

Conservative Progressivism?

An intriguing comparative study of security polices showed that in the past, liberal parties and coalitions worldwide have been able to use threats to national security to establish progressive tax reforms and a stronger state control over businesses and markets.[11] When the United States began its active participation in World War I, the country was witnessing an unprecedented concentration of federal power in Washington. Wilson justified this centralization as a temporary and necessary measure to provide efficiency to the government. Many new federal agencies had been established during the war, including the Fuel Administration, the Railroad War Board, the Food Administration, the War Industries Board, and many others. Agencies expanded the power of the federal government enormously. Wilson quadrupled the size of the Bureau of Internal Revenue to almost 16,000 employees. He established the Committee on Public Information to inform the public about government policies. The United States Employment Services provided workers to companies engaged in war contracts. Most of the war agencies had been dismantled in 1919–1920. Yet his policies provided sufficient background for the federal policies of the 1920s maintained by the Republican presidents Harding and Coolidge.

As a leader sharing basic progressive principles, Hughes believed that the federal government should play a significant role in the economic and social life of the country. The main question was about the depth and scope of such a role. Hughes was most suspicious about the ever-growing federal power. Compared to Wilson, who was relatively successful in federalizing so many policies during the war, Hughes would have been less enthusiastic to do the same. Therefore, he probably would have been less efficient as president on several domestic social policies because of his innate over-reliance on the free market.

As a progressive president, Hughes, like Wilson, would have sponsored education, low-interest loans to farmers, and antitrust policies.

Hughes would have supported state control of public utilities, retirement plans, labor safety laws, and protective legislation for children and women. As governor of New York, for example, he supported the eight-hour workday for railroad employees. Hughes would have supported the Nineteenth Amendment (stating that the right of citizens of the United States to vote shall not be denied because of sex). It was proposed on June 4, 1919, and ratified on August 18, 1920. However, tariffs on foreign trade or the passing of the Federal Reserve Act would have likely come to existence without Wilson being in power.

Conclusion

Hughes could have been the most influential and innovative Republican internationalist of the post-World War I era. As a realist with a vision of world stability, he would have redirected the attention of the Republican Party to international affairs and would have redefined America's position in world politics as a new leader. America under Hughes would have been an active member of the League of Nations, restraining some small "rough" states and planting the early seeds of interventionism around the world. Hughes might have postponed the confrontation with Japan but could not have prevented the Great Depression.

Hughes's commitment to limited government, private property, and individual liberty (presided over by common law judges) would not have allowed him to expand the federal bureaucracy to the limits reached by President Wilson. Hughes feared that bureaucratic power would subordinate law to its own ends, destroying individualism and political self-rule.[12] Hughes was decrying the enhanced power of the national state even at times of war, believing that bureaucracy has a tendency to grow and very seldom to shrink.

— 4 —

1960: KENNEDY DEFEATS NIXON— NO RECOUNTS

1960: The Election Year

Privately, many top Republicans wished they had not pushed in 1947 for the Twenty-second Amendment to the Constitution limiting the presidency to two terms. Dwight Eisenhower, who by the late 1950s was finishing his tenure in the White House, was widely respected as a war hero, and his name was comfortably associated with stability and peace. With passage of the amendment, however, and despite President Eisenhower's popularity, he could not run for a third term. The Republicans had to figure out how to win the presidency again without his name on the ballot. At the 1960 Republican National Convention in Chicago in July, Vice President Nixon was the overwhelming choice. Senator Barry Goldwater of Arizona, perceived as a more conservative candidate, received just ten delegate votes. Nixon then chose former Massachusetts senator and United Nations Ambassador Henry Cabot Lodge, Jr., as his vice presidential candidate. The nomination of Richard Nixon was a somewhat expected event; after all, he was the sitting vice president. His success as the party's top candidate was also rooted in other reasons. Nixon was a powerful representative of a young wing of the Republican Party who were born in the twentieth century. He was a forty-seven-year-old conservative with war experience and a law degree. Furthermore, he had distinguished himself on the national level first as a prominent member of the House and the Senate—where he was known as the staunch anti-communist who exposed Alger Hiss—and then as vice president under the popular Eisenhower.

The 1960 Democratic National Convention took place earlier in July in Los Angeles. After the primaries, Senator John Kennedy from Massachusetts appeared to be the clear frontrunner having defeated his influential opponents within the party, including Senator Hubert Humphrey. However, Kennedy had to face another challenge: two new candidates appeared right before the convention. One of them was Lyndon Johnson, the Senate Majority Leader from Texas, and Adlai Stevenson II, the Democratic Party candidate who lost in the 1952 and 1956 presidential elections. Yet Kennedy won the nomination on the first ballot and chose the fifty-two-year-old Lyndon Johnson as his running mate.

RESULTS OF THE 1960 PRESIDENTIAL ELECTION

Kennedy's victory on November 8 was exceptionally narrow. He defeated Nixon by 120 thousand votes out of 69 million cast. In the national popular vote, Kennedy beat Nixon by just one-tenth of one percentage point, which was the closest popular-vote margin of the twentieth century. Kennedy won eleven states by three percentage points or less, while Nixon carried five states by the same margin. The actual number of popular votes received by Kennedy is difficult to determine because of the unusual situation in Alabama and Georgia where the voters had to choose separate electors, some of whom did not have to pledge their votes for a specific candidate. Kennedy's success was greater in the Electoral College. Kennedy needed to win 269 votes. He received 303 electoral votes compared to Nixon's 219.

For more than half a century now, one of the most controversial aspects of the 1960 election are the returns from Illinois. Nixon won ninety-two downstate counties while Kennedy carried nine. Yet it was enough for Kennedy to win the state of Illinois by nine thousand votes.

Opinion polls had predicted a very close race between the candidates. According to the Gallup pre-election survey, about 52 percent of men preferred Kennedy and 48 supported Nixon. Women, in contrast, preferred Nixon by a 2-point margin: 51 against 49 percent. Kennedy did better (9–10 points) among voters younger than 49. Non-white voters by the margin 68-32 gave preference to Kennedy. Catholics voted

78-22 in favor of Kennedy. Union workers also gave support to Kennedy by a 65-35 margin.

Kennedy: Ten Chances to Lose the 1960 Election

Kennedy had placed a lot of emphasis on West Virginia, not because of the delegates at stake but for the symbolic value of a win in that state. He had entered the West Virginia primary to help silence those in his own party who did not believe that a Catholic could win a general election. Of course, if he lost in West Virginia it would have been seen as proof that the critics were correct. How crucial was this event in Kennedy's quest for presidency?

The general tendency of human memory is to retain the most vivid events and outstanding details. In a way, our memory is recording history in a similar fashion. Gradually, many presumably obscure facts, and seemingly unexciting developments fade away. As a result, our collective perception retains the images painted by bright strokes of our impressionable recollections and imagination. Many people who have some knowledge about the 1960 election perceive this contest as a victory of a young and vigorous Kennedy campaigning against an old and dull Nixon, although the age difference between them was only four years and Nixon did not appear particularly "boring" according to the 1960 polls. Kennedy was frequently portrayed during the campaign as the first would-be president born in the twentieth century (he was born in 1917). Nixon was born in 1913. Kennedy was a skillful tactician, efficient campaign manager, and persuasive debater. Nixon had comparable organizational qualities. Kennedy's campaign made several mistakes, so did Nixon's. Kennedy could have easily lost the election.

On the one hand, several facts suggest that Nixon, in theory, was destined to lose the contest. In the summer of 1960, polls and voter registration statistics revealed that Democrats outnumbered Republicans by several million. Thus, Kennedy's campaign always took pains to stress that he was a Democrat and Nixon a Republican. While Eisenhower was still popular as president, the 1958 midterm elections had brought overwhelming Democratic majorities to the House and Senate. By that time

Republicans retained only seventeen governorships out of fifty. Democratic resurgence was due largely to the recession of 1958, which the country was only beginning to come out of in 1960. To win, Nixon had to persuade almost a quarter of Democrats to switch, and at the same time, retain more than a half of independent votes. That was a tall order.

On the other hand, a general theory of electoral behavior also suggests that Kennedy's chances to lose the election—despite all the statistical comparisons—were greater than Nixon's. Most senior Democratic leaders, including former President Truman, saw Kennedy's youth and inexperience as a huge liability. Many southerners were hesitant to vote for a Yankee. Moreover, he was a Catholic, and anti-Catholic prejudice in the country was assumed to be a serious obstacle to winning a national election. He could not have taken the minority vote for granted as he did not campaign vigorously on the civil rights platform, especially in the southern states.

At the beginning of the campaign, it looked like the stars were not aligning for Kennedy. Nixon and his camp did everything slightly better. The Republican Convention in Chicago seemed to demonstrate stability and strength of the Grand Old Party. Most observers liked Nixon's acceptance speech better than Kennedy's Democratic Convention speech. Nixon's choice for vice president—U.S. Ambassador to the United Nations Cabot Lodge—seemed more inspiring than Kennedy's choice of Lyndon Johnson. Johnson was from the South and could have brought extra votes, yet Lodge had an advantage in terms of his foreign policy experience. On the Senate floor, Kennedy frequently appeared weak. Even in the majority, Democrats in the Senate were frequently stymied by their own conservative Democratic senators who more often than not voted with the Republicans. There were always veto threats from the White House.

Still, Kennedy did manage a campaign that portrayed him as the vigorous war hero. His wartime story, as told in the tale of PT-109 (his motor torpedo boat), was skillfully used to make character a central campaign issue. Could anything have prevented his victory?

1960 Presidential Election
State-by-State Popular and Electoral College Vote

State	John F. Kennedy (Democrat, MA)			Richard M. Nixon (Republican, CA)		
	Vote	%	ECV	Vote	%	ECV
ALABAMA	318,303	56.8	5	236,110	42.1	-
ALASKA	29,809	49.1	-	30,953	50.9	3
ARIZONA	176,781	44.4	-	221,241	55.5	4
ARKANSAS	215,049	50.2	8	184,508	43.1	-
CALIFORNIA	3,224,099	49.6	-	3,259,722	50.1	32
COLORADO	330,629	44.9	-	402,242	54.6	6
CONNECTICUT	657,055	53.7	8	565,813	46.3	-
DELAWARE	99,590	50.6	3	96,373	49	-
FLORIDA	748,700	48.5	-	795,476	51.5	10
GEORGIA	458,638	62.5	12	274,472	37.4	-
HAWAII	92,410	50	3	92,295	50	-
IDAHO	138,853	46.2	-	161,597	53.8	4
ILLINOIS	2,377,846	50	27	2,368,988	49.8	-
INDIANA	952,358	44.6	-	1,175,120	55	13
IOWA	550,565	43.2	-	722,381	56.7	10
KANSAS	363,213	39.1	-	561,474	60.5	8
KENTUCKY	521,855	46.4	-	602,607	53.6	10
LOUISIANA	407,339	50.4	10	230,980	28.6	-
MAINE	181,159	43	-	240,608	57.1	5
MARYLAND	565,808	53.6	9	489,538	46.4	-
MASSACHUSETTS	1,487,174	60.2	16	976,750	39.6	-
MICHIGAN	1,687,269	50.9	20	1,620,428	48.8	-
MINNESOTA	779,933	50.6	11	757,915	49.2	-
MISSISSIPPI	108,362	36.3	-	73,561	24.7	—
MISSOURI	972,201	50.3	13	962,218	49.7	-
MONTANA	134,891	48.6	-	141,841	51.1	4
NEBRASKA	232,542	37.9	-	380,553	62.1	6
NEVADA	54,880	51.2	3	52,387	48.8	-
NEW HAMPSHIRE	137,772	46.6	-	157,989	53.4	4
NEW JERSEY	1,385,415	50	16	1,363,324	49.2	-
NEW MEXICO	156,027	50.2	4	153,733	49.4	-
NEW YORK	3,830,085	52.5	45	3,446,419	47.3	-
N. CAROLINA	713,136	52.1	14	655,420	47.9	-
N. DAKOTA	123,963	44.5	-	154,310	55.4	4
OHIO	1,944,248	46.7	-	2,217,611	53.3	25
OKLAHOMA	370,111	41	-	533,039	59	7
OREGON	367,402	47.3	-	408,065	52.6	6
PENNSYLVANIA	2,556,282	51.1	32	2,439,956	48.7	-
RHODE ISLAND	258,032	63.6	4	147,502	36.4	-
S. CAROLINA	198,121	51.2	8	188,558	48.8	-
S. DAKOTA	128,070	41.8	-	178,417	58.2	4
TENNESSEE	481,453	45.8	-	556,577	52.9	11
TEXAS	1,167,935	50.5	24	1,121,693	48.5	-
UTAH	169,248	45.2	-	205,361	54.8	4
VERMONT	69,186	41.4	-	98,131	58.7	3
VIRGINIA	362,327	47	-	404,521	52.4	12
WASHINGTON	599,298	48.3	-	629,273	50.7	9
WEST VIRGINIA	441,786	52.7	8	395,995	47.3	-
WISCONSIN	830,805	48.1	-	895,175	51.8	12
WYOMING	63,331	45	-	77,451	55	3
	34,221,344	49.7	303	34,106,671	49.5	219

A slate of "unpledged" Electoral College candidates polled 39.0% of the vote in Mississippi, carrying the state. Mississippi's eight Electoral College votes were cast for Harry F. Byrd of Virginia, who also received six Electoral College votes from Alabama and one from Oklahoma.

EISENHOWER REMAINS POPULAR

Political scientist Lee Sigelman underlines the importance of a direct connection between presidential popularity a few months before the election and the outcome of the vote even if the incumbent is not on the ballot. It means that all negative perceptions associated with the incumbent president are very likely to be attributed to his party's candidate. This was particularly true in the case of Nixon, who spent eight years in the Eisenhower administration and could not escape criticism for the mistakes made in the White House during that time. Several tactical errors or unlucky developments turned votes away from Nixon, especially those of the undecided and first-time voters. Some facts remain well known while others fade away in obscurity. Nevertheless, they all have contributed to a certain degree to Nixon's eventual defeat in November.

One of the most profound rules of a candidate's political campaign is to avoid making obvious mistakes. Eisenhower, although he did not run for the presidency, committed at least one such blunder rather unintentionally. When a reporter asked the president in August if he could think of any advice for Nixon that he, the president, had heeded, Eisenhower threw out his infamous, "If you give me a week I might think of one." It looked like Eisenhower was trying to be informal with the media. Conversely, the president wanted to appear independent in his political decisions and did not want to give an impression that somebody else was in charge of his important actions. Whatever Eisenhower meant by the comment, Nixon's political opponents quickly called him a negligible "factor" or an empty suit in the White House. It is difficult to estimate how many votes were lost as a result of the comments, but in an election this close even a few make the difference. In late October, President Eisenhower began a campaign tour for Nixon, which gave him a boost in opinion polls. Obviously, it was not enough to secure the victory.

KENNEDY CHOOSES THE WRONG PLATFORM

For his part, Kennedy could have made several tactical errors. First,

Kennedy could have failed to capitalize on the phenomenon known today as "incumbent fatigue" (or "the voters' term limits"). The fatigue is manifest through the voters' general inclination to replace the incumbent, not necessarily or exclusively because of the voter's political or ideological views, but primarily because of the electorate's weariness with the current official. This was an important fact contributing to President George H.W. Bush's loss in 1992 and Al Gore's defeat in 2000. Electoral studies show that incumbency, in general, should help a candidate representing the "old" regime unless the incumbency was associated with a major disaster or a scandal. Incumbency, nonetheless, is not necessarily a sure "positive" factor contributing to reelection. Many voters tend to believe an incumbent stays in office for too long. If Kennedy had failed to build an image of a man who could move the country forward, he could have lost the election. He persuaded the people that America needed a new push; it was sitting too long on a cozy cushion of self-satisfaction and stagnation on both the domestic and international front.

Second, Kennedy could have focused on his legislative and political record and explored comparisons between his own and Nixon's records in the Senate. In this type of tactical struggle over the question, "Whose legislative record is better?" Kennedy would have lost. Voters can use at least two strategies to evaluate candidates. In prospective evaluations, people assess the ability of the candidate to fulfill his or her promises if elected to the office. In retrospective evaluations, the public considers how the candidate performed in the past. While focusing on ambitious promises, and building his image as a young politician committed to change, Kennedy ignited prospective evaluations and gathered additional votes that could have determined the result of the election.

Third, Kennedy could have pushed actively for civil rights legislation. This most likely would have cost him several southern states. Historians even say, for example, that Robert Kennedy, who ran his brother's campaign, criticized JFK for placing a call to Coretta Scott King, wife of Martin Luther King, Jr., right before the election. News of this phone call could have cost him many southern votes.

Fourth, Kennedy could have chosen a more liberal-progressive political platform, which could have also cost him some decisive votes. Supporting labor unions, various government programs, and other traditional liberal policies, he remained solid about several issues that gave him the decisive votes of social conservatives. In particular, he was actively campaigning for a stronger national defense and for a more active government role in defense research and manufacturing. As an example, if Kennedy did not secure enough conservative Catholic and Jewish votes in New York, he could have lost 45 electoral votes (Kennedy won by 384,000 votes out of more than 7.2 million cast). As a result, the next president would have been Nixon.

IMAGE-BUILDING BACKFIRES

Kennedy could have easily overplayed his image-building strategy and turned off many voters. The election year of 1960 was the beginning of the period that historians frequently label the age of "new politics." In the continuum between substance and style, the latter was becoming more important for political candidates, campaign managers, and voters. In this new age of television, both candidates tried to appeal to voters directly. This meant that politicians had to pay much greater and serious attention to how they looked, spoke, gestured, and answered questions. Electoral studies repeatedly show that the most partisan voters will vote for their party's candidate under almost any circumstance regardless of the candidate's platform. In other cases, the image of the candidate can make a difference among moderate, undecided, or gullible voters. In 1964, Philip Converse's seminal article titled, "The Nature of Belief Systems in Mass Publics," showed that for many people, their strong political convictions and party affiliations are rooted in emotional factors, exciting experiences, or convenient assumptions.[1]

In 1960, both candidates tried to differentiate themselves from each other. Nixon tried wherever possible to underline similarities between himself and Kennedy on several key domestic issues and the necessity of building up the nation's defenses to resist the Soviet Union. However, Nixon's campaign also focused on his experience in domestic and foreign affairs, contrasting that record with Kennedy's inexperience. The

Kennedy camp focused on a dynamic change. Nixon, from their point of view, was not capable of moving the country forward. On October 25, in one of the campaign speeches in Aurora, Illinois, Kennedy emphasized the difference between himself and his opponent: "You have to make your decision of what you want this country to be. What you want Illinois to be. How ready you are to move this country forward? That is the question which separates Mr. Nixon and myself." This was a message that Kennedy repeated continuously and in different ways. Moreover, Kennedy was actively building his image by portraying himself not only as active, but also as a caring person ready to move on in contrast to a stagnant and uncaring bureaucrat Nixon. Pointing out direct associations between Nixon and the old president, Eisenhower, became very convenient. Kennedy was deliberately contrasting his own activist stance with that of the aging former general, who appeared to depend so heavily on the individuals and committees advising him. Emphasizing the challenges ahead, Kennedy called his domestic program the "New Frontier." He was portraying himself as a young leader ready to break with the past and to offer new solutions to old problems. Kennedy ambitiously promised generous federal funding for education, medical care for the elderly, and government intervention in case of economic recession.

Kennedy became an early master at presenting visuals and spent hundreds of thousands of dollars to hire a film crew and equip a bus to film all of his public appearances. The footage then would appear as part of Kennedy's television advertising campaign. This highly professional approach created a sense that genuine excitement accompanied all of Kennedy's public appearances.[2] By and large, the Nixon campaign did not seem to understand how campaigning had changed in a few short years. Certainly Nixon learned from his 1960 experience, because in 1968 he demonstrated a masterful command of the new campaign style.

Overall, according to historian and political psychologist James Barber, Nixon could have won if he better accentuated Kennedy's three potential liabilities: his relative immaturity, his partisan commitment (was he a true liberal or moderately conservative?), and Kennedy's super-competitiveness or feistiness (which could have been portrayed as a negative feature of a president overshadowing reason and restraint in policy-making, especially in dangerous situations). Nixon's basic campaign theme—maturity and experience to cope with the Soviet Union—failed to stir any significant surge among the voters.[3]

NIXON REJECTS TV DEBATES

On September 26, during the first televised debates between presidential candidates in U.S. history, Nixon appeared, according to surveys of television audiences, tired, restrained, and nervous, compared to his younger-looking opponent. Kennedy's preparation for the debates included resting a few days in Florida—thus the natural suntan. Nixon, however, came to the debates from a round of intense campaigning. Nixon also endured the first debate under some significant pain having injured his knee getting out of the car. The injury was severe enough that later on he was sidelined for a few days. Interestingly enough, those who saw the debates on television tended to see Kennedy as the victor—not surprising given Kennedy's attention to the role of the camera and his understanding of the importance of visual presentation. Nevertheless, those who listened to the debates on the radio were more likely to consider Nixon, not Kennedy as the winner. As a defeated Nixon came to believe, "The visual wins over the verbal; the eye predominates over the ear; sight beats sound."

By agreeing to the debates, Nixon gave Kennedy, an upstart senator, the opportunity to appear at the same level as the vice president of the United States. The debates gave Kennedy a chance to prove to the nation that he could be as logical, persuasive, calm, and forceful as Vice President Nixon. He was a perfect challenger and a great match. Kennedy, of course, could have done much worse in the debates, but he did not. In sum, if Nixon had refused to debate in October, his chances of winning would have been improved.

YOUNG VOTERS REMAIN UNINSPIRED

An interesting assumption about Kennedy's potential loss comes from studies of voting behavior. Young voters and first-time voters contribute significantly to the most decisive victories in presidential elections. The generational groups—people of the same age—tend to maintain relatively stable partisan attachments despite political fluctuations in the country. The shift in party identification is likely to be caused by the younger age cohorts: they bring new balance to party affiliations. During the years of Republican presidencies (for example, the Eisenhower years between 1952 and 1956), more young people voted for the Republican Party than did any other age group. Similarly, during the "Democratic" years (after 1960), more young people than in any other age group formed their identification with the Democratic Party. In other words, the young had a substantial impact on the outcome of the 1960 vote. If Kennedy had failed to ignite the younger voters, he could have easily lost the election.

Preachers Do Not Intervene

On September 7, a group of 150 prominent Protestant clergymen and activists met in Washington to declare their opposition to a Catholic presidential candidate. If this event did not take place or if it did not receive serious publicity, Nixon might have become president. Why?

That Kennedy was Catholic was widely considered as his substantial liability. When he was nominated, even some of his supporters expressed grave doubts that a Catholic could win; after all, in 1928 Al Smith, the only other Catholic to run for president, had been soundly defeated. Why should the Democrats repeat the same mistake in 1960? Opponents openly asked where Kennedy's loyalties resided. Would he report to the Pope in the Vatican to receive policy directions and other specific "orders"? Generally, warm and enthusiastic feelings for the young senator were tempered by strong doubts and prejudice. Back in the late 1950s, according to polls, almost a quarter of American voters expressed a reluctant attitude about a Catholic presidential candidate.

Similar doubts about the electability of a non-Protestant will continue to emerge for many years to come. When Senator Joseph Lieberman—who is an Orthodox Jew—was chosen for the vice-presidential nomination for the Democratic Party in August 2000, quite a few commentators raised their concerns about whether the senator, if elected, would put interests of his religion and the state of Israel before the interests of American people. In 2008, many voters viewed Mormon Mitt Romney's religious affiliation as a serious issue, which probably contributed to his failure during the primaries. In general, after the 1970s, national surveys show that increased majority percentages of Americans considered religious affiliation of a presidential candidate as a non-factor in their voting decisions.[4]

By 1960, the percentage of the U.S. population identifying itself as Catholic had reached 24 percent. In theory, Kennedy could have secured almost a quarter of the electorate, and that might have been a crucial factor contributing to his victory. Statistically, the Catholic population was concentrated heavily in three key states, that is, those with high Electoral College votes—Massachusetts, New Jersey, and New York—that today comprise 40–50 percent of Catholic voters in the country. Back in 1960, altogether, the victory in these three states gave Kennedy seventy-seven electoral votes (as you remember, he defeated Nixon by eighty-four votes). Without the Catholic vote, he would have lost badly. It is very likely that Kennedy's centrist position on many issues helped to sway many conservative Catholics to vote for his candidacy.

Why did the Washington meeting play such an important role in Kennedy's victory? During this meeting, it was stated that electing a Catholic could create a dangerous precedent. Although many participants later commented that that meeting was largely theological and did not intend to pressure the voters, the criticism had already spread across the country. Feeling prejudice and discrimination, many conservative Catholics, who initially leaned toward Nixon, began to support Kennedy, thus bringing the votes of many urban centers to the Kennedy's camp. Kennedy also tried to address his views on religion and politics directly. On September 12, he gave a speech before a meeting of Protestant ministers in Houston, Texas. He promised to obey the principle of the separation of church and state. He also promised to not consent to Catholic clergy if they attempted to influence his policies.

Very often, certain political actions backfire. In our case, the "Washington statement" by the conservative Protestants gave Kennedy additional ammunition: a backlash from many Catholics switching away from Nixon, and Kennedy's opportunity to emphasize a non-political role of religion in America.

THE "MISSILE GAP" IS NOT MENTIONED

One of the key phrases that Kennedy repeated during the campaign was "the missile gap." This meant, according to Kennedy, that the Soviets had surpassed America in manufacturing and deploying nuclear missiles. Kennedy advisers later acknowledged that the missile gap mantra was somewhat exaggerated. His opponents complained that it was a lie, but it was too late. Eisenhower addressed the gap (specifically, the absence of it) in person but only on Kennedy's inauguration day. It was true that Soviet leader Nikita Khrushchev was making serious plans to modernize the Soviet military and to improve his country's missile programs drastically. Yet in 1960, as facts clearly suggest today, there was no real missile gap between Washington and Moscow, the Cold War chief rivals. However, the criticisms of the old defense policy apparently worked in Kennedy's favor: they came to symbolize the complacency of the Eisenhower administration and the lack of presidential leadership. Again, the entire issue of national defense became tied to the general perception of passivity on the part of Eisenhower's cabinet.

KENNEDY IGNORES HARRIS

The 1960 campaign was one of the earliest in history in which the candidates could have used reliable public opinion polls based on representative samples and conducted via telephone. (In fact, the polls accurately predicted a very narrow victory for Kennedy.) Kennedy could have lost the election if he did not use polls in his campaign. Kennedy paid constant attention to the issues most popular with voters. Political scientists Lawrence Jacobs and Robert Shapiro found that JFK and his staff carefully followed the opinion polls.[5] His advisers, one of whom was Louis Harris, the founder of Harris Polls, studied national surveys and prepared questions for Kennedy's press conferences and debates to identify the most important issues reflected in these surveys. Specifically, there were at least seven themes reflected in the polls: increasing Social Security, passing Medicare legislation, reforming education, fighting unemployment, combating the high cost of living, increasing military spending, and bolstering U.S. prestige around the world. An analysis of his speeches made in October shows that at the end of his campaign, Kennedy's positions on these issues and the public views were the closest. For instance, a major increase of people's anxiety about worsening unemployment expressed in the polls is matched with the noteworthy increase in Kennedy's references to unemployment in his speeches. Overall, Kennedy was highly responsive to the issues that were highly salient to people at a given moment. Nixon's speeches, though, did not reflect immediate fluctuations of public opinion.

NIXON DOES NOT CAMPAIGN IN ALL FIFTY STATES

Another possible costly mistake was Nixon's promise to campaign in all fifty states. While a tough campaign fighter who did not mind the grueling schedule and nonstop appearances, he paid a high price for the promise. Campaigning in "banner districts"—districts, cities, and states in which victory is almost guaranteed—wastes time and resources. Instead, a candidate should focus most effort on the district where the electoral results are expected to be close. In addition, Nixon had sustained an injury to his knee and had to take a time out from his traveling schedule to return to Washington for treatment. Nixon's critics claimed that his stubbornness did not allow his campaign to focus on the most crucial states, such as Illinois or Michigan, which he eventually lost by slim margins. In the last two weeks of campaigning in October, Nixon visited eleven states, seven of which he lost. Except for Ohio (Nixon won) and New York (Kennedy won), the margin of victory was 1 to 2 percentage points or less.

NIXON CONTESTS THE ELECTION

In a recorded 1983 interview, Nixon said that he believed he had won Illinois and Texas in 1960. He lost because there was "immense fraud," particularly in Illinois. Why did Nixon choose to concede the race? Kennedy won in the Electoral College. However, it was clear that Nixon had a moral right to contest. For example, most of the states voted in his favor. Most voters from several main social categories, including women, college graduates, Protestant voters, and senior citizens, did not vote for Kennedy. Yet Nixon said that he chose not to contest the results, because it would have had a disruptive effect on the country, leaving the United States without a president for months. In addition, it would have set a bad international example and would have sent a wrong message to countries struggling toward democracy. Nixon also alleged that if Kennedy lost the election, the senator might have acted differently and challenged the results of the vote.

For years to come, textbooks will keep mentioning electoral returns from Illinois as one of the most controversial issues of the 1960 election. Kennedy won in nine counties there. Nixon was victorious in ninety-two. Yet, in terms of absolute numbers, Kennedy carried this state by some 9,000 votes. His victory in Illinois came from the city of Chicago. Mayor Richard J. Daley held back much of Chicago's vote until the late morning hours of November 9. The efforts of Daley and the powerful Chicago Democratic organization gave Kennedy an extraordinary Cook County victory margin of 450,000 votes, thus overcoming the heavy Republican vote downstate. Nixon opponents have a strong argument: the Republican-dominated State Board of Elections unanimously rejected the challenge to the results. The case is closed.

Another argument is that if we look carefully at the numbers, we should see that Illinois alone could not have changed the general electoral outcome. If Nixon had successfully challenged the results, he would have received 246 electoral votes, but that would have still left him trailing Kennedy by 30 votes. To ensure victory, Nixon should have challenged the results, for example, from Texas, which he had lost by 46,000 votes. In fact, Nixon believed that in both Illinois and Texas the most egregious fraud took place. In addition to these states, Hawaii and Alabama are also frequently mentioned as two potentially winnable appeals that Nixon might have filed.

Now imagine that Nixon decided to go ahead and contest the electoral results in several states. If the Illinois or Texas results were reversed, he would have needed a similar reversal in just one more relatively big state to get the majority of electoral votes. Nixon mentioned Missouri or South Carolina, which he lost by a slim margin of ten thousand votes each. In 2000, Al Gore challenged the results in Florida and lost in court. Nixon did not challenge, and yet if he did, he could have won. If history turned that way, today we would have remembered the term, "the 1960 Illinois recount."

If Kennedy Were Not Elected

What role did Kennedy play in history? What would have happened had he not been elected president? Did it actually matter who became president in 1960?

No "Whiz Kids"

Kennedy brought more than just "nine strangers and a brother for a Cabinet," as one of his aides jokingly remarked.[6] Many people brought to the administration or working closely with Kennedy contributed to the growing perception of the youth and energy associated with the new administration. Robert McNamara, secretary of defense, was forty-four. The president's younger brother, Robert Kennedy who was thirty-five, became attorney general. Byron White, who was forty-two, served as U.S. deputy attorney general; he was later appointed to the Supreme Court. Another Supreme Court Justice appointed by Kennedy, Arthur J. Goldberg, was fifty-two when he became secretary of labor. Kennedy's brother-in-law Sargent Shriver took over the Peace Corps at forty-five. Stewart L. Udall, secretary of the interior, was forty. Orville L. Freeman, secretary of agriculture, one of the designers of the food stamp program, was forty-two. C. Douglas Dillon, secretary of the treasury, was fifty-one. Secretary of State Dean Rusk was fifty-one. Most of his close colleagues and staff members went through college in the 1930s, many in the Northeast. There were at least ten Rhodes Scholars among the members of Kennedy's inner circle.

Most people who served close to Kennedy served in World War II (1941–1945). Their spirit of relentless effort and pragmatic idealism defined this New Frontier generation. As historian Anna Nelson argues, the staffing policies of Robert McNamara and McGeorge Bundy that brought the "whiz kids" to the Defense Department and youthful assistants to the National Security Council staff may have obscured the importance of the old hands, whose vested interest in the old policies has yet to be fully explored.[7] Kennedy did use the services of several "dinosaurs" of U.S. foreign policy, including sixty-five-year-olds Adolph Berle and Paul Nitze, sixty-seven-year-old Dean Acheson, and sixty-nine-year-old Averell Harriman. But for the most part, Kennedy brought to power a young, dynamic group of people who influenced American domestic and foreign policy for many years after his death.

Meet Nixon's Appointees

Who would have joined the Nixon cabinet? There could have been Nixon's senior campaign lieutenants such as Secretary of Labor James Mitchell, Attorney General William Rogers (who served under Nixon later), and Secretary of the Interior Fred Seaton. Most likely, there could have been Robert H. Finch, who managed Nixon's 1960 presidential campaign and later served as his secretary of health, education, and welfare. However, there would not have been Henry Kissinger in the cabinet (although Kissinger was already advising Nelson Rockefeller who years later suggested him to Nixon). Nelson Rockefeller could have joined as secretary of state or in some other role as a senior adviser on foreign policy. There was much campaign hype about appointing a black person to a cabinet post, although Nixon insisted that he would "appoint the best man possible without regard to race, creed or color." Nixon was planning a new position to head an institution for economic affairs, the status of which would resemble that of the National Security Council.

Domestic Policies: Business as Usual

As vice president, Nixon attended most of the councils of the

Eisenhower administration. Nixon presided at meetings of the cabinet and the National Security Council when Eisenhower was absent. As president, Nixon would have faced a somewhat manageable Congress from 1961 to 1962. The Democrats won 262 seats compared to the Republicans' 174. In the Senate, the 65-35 majority appeared decisive compared to today's standards. Nevertheless, conservative Democrats and Republicans together outnumbered Kennedy supporters of the progressive wing. A sizable portion of Democratic senators voted consistently with the thirty-five Republicans, particularly on matters related to social issues. Kennedy distanced himself from the civil rights movement, and was thus seen by some of its leaders as unsupportive of their efforts. Nixon was not expected to be supportive. Facing a lukewarm attitude from Congress, Nixon would have approached domestic policy from a moderate, non-ideological platform. After all, before he became vice president, his record in Congress reflected his conservative attitudes about the central question of the government's role in national life, even though he held somewhat liberal views on civil rights.

A Different Defense Policy

In early 1961, impelled by the need to separate themselves from the Eisenhower era, Kennedy and Defense Secretary McNamara moved decisively and quickly to make changes in defense policies. "Indecision itself results, in effect, in endorsing previous policy decisions," McNamara asserted. Rapidly, budgets were amended to accelerate the construction of Polaris submarines and Minuteman missiles and to expand the ability to fight limited wars by increasing funds for conventional weapons, such as armored cars, transport planes, and electronic equipment. A counterinsurgency program to combat Soviet military support for "national liberation" movements was substantially enlarged. In three years, the Kennedy defense buildup resulted in about $17 billion in additional appropriations.[8]

There is no serious reason to expect that Nixon would have been indecisive in defense policies. Opinion polls at that time supported the view that the United States should have had military superiority over the

Soviets. Defense spending also meant job security for millions of Americans. Yet Nixon did not have to prove anything immediately by challenging his predecessor's defense policy. As part of the previous administration, he needed to maintain an image of continuation. Kennedy was different.

A DISSIMILAR SPACE PROGRAM

After the successful launches of the first Sputnik satellite in October 1957 and the first manned flight in April 1961, the Soviet government had a psychological momentum on its side. The successful space program was like an injection of optimism and a morale boost for the Soviet people. It also reflected the growing sense of confidence and even superiority in the Kremlin about its military and nuclear capabilities. Kennedy's interest in space programs was not just a desire to initiate a policy. He wanted to win over the Soviets. A new space program reflected his personal effect. To competitive Kennedy, the space program was a personal challenge, which he eagerly accepted. He asked Vice President Johnson (who was appointed to chair the President's Committee for Science) to come up with a plan that would put America first as a space explorer. Johnson steered the recommendation toward an ambitious program for landing an American on the moon.

Nixon as president in 1961 would likely have developed a new space program as well. There is little doubt that the need for such a program was clearly understood in the White House and Congress. This program would have been less competitive and ambitious under Nixon though. Space competition was not Nixon's top priority, and he did not have any grand desires to compete against the Soviets in the stratosphere.

The Cold War space competition continued through the 1960s and beyond. Later, trying to match Kennedy and Johnson's ambitious project, the Soviets planned to attempt a similar Moon landing program, but later switched to sending electronic "robots on wheels" to explore the Moon's surface. Nevertheless, cooperation between the two countries began. The Soviet leader Nikita Khrushchev agreed to a Soviet-U.S. joint space venture in 1963, which resulted in the first joint Apollo-Soyuz space mission twelve years later, in 1975. Similar joint international space missions continue today.

FOREIGN POLICY WITHOUT HENRY KISSINGER

During the election campaign, Nixon was frequently portrayed by Kennedy as a "trigger-happy" politician who could easily set off a major war by initiating minor confrontations with the communist opponents, especially in Southeast Asia. Yet Nixon would have probably based his foreign policy on his traditional personal and administrative strengths or successful habits. Among such habits were a tendency to negotiate in secrecy; a desire to rely on a very small circle of close advisers; a growing understanding of the necessity to reach a balance in international relations by allowing the Soviets to retain certain areas of influence; and agreeing on particular rules of international conduct. Ideology would have played a lesser role in U.S. foreign policy in exchange for pragmatic calculations and diplomatic deals. Nixon would have continued, like Eisenhower, to support regimes friendly to America all over the world. Although, as president, Kennedy was concerned that neglect of the nationalist and anti-colonial movements would force America to turn to communist leadership and the Soviet Union, in reality neither president had many choices in his foreign policy regarding the developing world.

Like Kennedy, Nixon was influenced by the old elites that dominated during the eight years of the Eisenhower administration. With or without Kissinger by his side, Nixon had already had enough experience in foreign policy before 1960. Nixon had made nine official trips abroad as vice president. In Congress, he had shown his strong anti-communist attitudes and support for foreign aid to states friendly to the United States. Most probably, Nixon would have restructured his foreign policy decision-making process. Most decisions made in the Eisenhower administration were heavily dependent on various committees and experts. This was a serious weakness underlined by Kennedy during his presidential campaign, and Nixon was very well aware of that. Like Kennedy, Nixon would have relied on a small group of close advisers to make important decisions especially during a crisis. For example, very early in his presidency, Kennedy rapidly dismantled the vast and complicated structure of the National Security Council and created a new, more efficient one. Nixon would have moved in a similar direction. The reliance on a small group of close advisers and staff is now a common feature of foreign-policy decision-making procedures for American presidents.

Partially, and as an attempt at continuing to change the structures and procedures left from the previous administration, Kennedy pursued rapid changes in military strategies. He wanted to provide quick and decisive responses against insurgency all over the world. This policy was called "flexible response." One of the major results of it was the rapid expansion of U.S. armed forces including combat-ready armored divisions and nuclear submarines.

Under Nixon, America would not have had the Peace Corps. The idea of having an official institution to send young and enthusiastic Americans overseas to promote peace, democracy, and freedom was discussed in Congress and supported by some private organizations. Yet Nixon did not like that particular idea. This new organization, as he thought, would attract primarily unskilled individuals and adventurists and would not do much to improve America's image abroad. Nixon also would not have supported the Alliance for Progress, Kennedy's proposed $100 billion partnership with Latin American governments.

Nixon could have tried to explore the Chinese card, but nothing resembling the diplomatic breakthrough of the 1970s would ever have happened at that time. Several reasons should explain this view. The tensions between the Soviet Union and China were mounting in the early 1960s, but they did not translate into open hostilities that took place later in the decade. Only in the 1970s did Nixon take advantage of the Soviet-Chinese rift by approaching the communist government. The policies of the Great Leap Forward and the Cultural Revolution did not provide an accommodating political climate within the communist administration of Chairman Mao. They would not have welcomed the U.S. president. Moreover, in the early 1960s, Nixon would not have allowed the seating of Communist China in the United Nations.

INTERNATIONAL CRISES

There is little reason to believe that Nixon would have confronted international crises differently than Kennedy did. JFK as president confronted at least three major international crises. Each of them could have triggered a nuclear conflict between Washington and Moscow: the Berlin crisis of 1961, the Bay of Pigs invasion of 1961, and the Cuban missile crisis of 1962. In all three cases, Kennedy's major accomplishment was that he avoided, despite several critical developments, a major military confrontation with the Soviet Union.

Nixon could not have prevented the Cuban leadership from turning to the Soviet Union and adopting the communist ideology as a source of its policies. Although President Eisenhower is commonly blamed for paying little attention to the young Cuban leader Fidel Castro and not taking him seriously, still, by the beginning of the would-be Nixon term in the White House, Cuba had pledged its friendship to Moscow. Perhaps Nixon would have been less confrontational with Castro, yet he would not have had a desire to back off. A vast majority of his advisers would have suggested a very tough approach against the communist government in Havana.

Nixon also would not have prevented the Berlin crisis and stopped the Soviet Union from building a "security fence" around West Berlin, the action that effectively isolated the city from the rest of the world. However, Nixon could have reduced the tensions by agreeing to make West Berlin an international city in 1961. This was a real possibility, because Nixon would not have worried about appearing weak while conducting his European and Soviet policies. Almost a decade later, an international agreement on the status of West Berlin had been signed approving its special status. Politically, ideologically, and economically, however, Berlin remained de facto a part of the West.

Supporters of a confrontational approach could easily argue today that all the tensions around Berlin in the 1960s played a special role in the history of the Cold War. The Berlin Wall became an unpopular symbol of ideological confrontation and communist oppression. The existence of the wall did not improve the image of the Soviet Union and the international communist system in general. In fact, the Berlin Wall had made a symbolic contribution to the ending of the Cold War. It was a painful thorn in the body of communism, such that an early resolution of the Berlin crisis would have delayed the ending of communism in the Soviet Union and in Eastern Europe in the mid-1980s.

THE CUBAN MISSILE CRISIS

Could Nixon have prevented the Cuban missile crisis? Most likely not. The delayed reaction of Washington to the appearance of nuclear missiles in Cuba was based on technical capabilities to detect such weapons. Kennedy complained privately that he "inherited" incompetent intelligence and military advisers from Eisenhower. John McCone replaced the CIA director Allen Dulles in November 1961. Could Nixon then have negotiated with the Soviets from the beginning to strike a deal of some sort? Because he knew the Soviet leader Nikita Khrushchev personally, could there have been a better line of communication established between Moscow and Washington from the beginning of the conflict? There are several answers to these questions.

Most historians of the Cold War admit today that the Cuban missile crisis was overall a failure of Soviet policies. Moscow leadership realized that it should never approach the United States again from the position of weakness. Responding to Kennedy's tough actions during the crisis, the leaders in Moscow pushed for a nuclear arms race. The response to Kennedy's actions was also a personal challenge for Khrushchev. He thought that Kennedy was a weak leader, worse yet a spoiled kid from Massachusetts. Therefore, the experienced and self-righteous Soviet leader could not afford to be pushed around by a "youngster." A new position of relative parity in nuclear capabilities would have given Moscow considerable strength in international relations. Had Nixon negotiated during the missile crisis, the Soviets might not have pushed for an unprecedented arms buildup in the 1960s. In other words, the Cuban missile negotiations might have prevented the most dangerous confrontation to date and served as a good lesson for future cooperation between the world's two superpowers. Yet this option is criticized by supporters of the view that the Soviet Union considered the military competition with the United States as an ideological issue, a reflection of the most fundamental goals of their foreign policy at the time. No matter what Nixon did or didn't do, the Soviets would have pushed forward believing that their economic and military development were the clear signs of their superiority over the West.

THE BAY OF PIGS NEVER TAKES PLACE

Nixon could have avoided some obvious mistakes committed by Kennedy and his closest advisers. There is more than a sufficient sample of memoirs, analyses, and interviews suggesting that Kennedy together with Dean Rusk, Robert McNamara, Douglas Dillon, McGeorge Bundy, and Robert Kennedy went along with the Bay of Pigs invasion arrangement despite the plan's obvious errors. Why did such an obvious mistake happen? Political psychologists believe that this was a perfect example of the so-called groupthink phenomenon, which is based on a collective assumption that it is better to make a collective decision than to facilitate group tensions and provoke continuous disagreements among the participants. Specifically, Kennedy's closest advisers simply went along with the president's ambitious plans and did not warn him about the possible disastrous consequences. Nixon, though, because of his emphasis on secrecy and straightforward assessments, could have avoided the groupthink mistakes and could have made fewer tactical errors preparing the operation. In fact, Nixon was in favor of an invasion by exile Cubans when he was vice president. He was pleased with the efforts of the U.S. government to assist the rebel forces with training, ammunition, and supplies.

Nevertheless, there are only a handful of people who would insist that an invasion against Cuba would have been successful at that time. The revolution led by Fidel Castro was supported by the majority of the Cuban population. If Nixon understood how insignificant the chances for success were, he would have scrapped or postponed the plans for a military intervention. Moreover, because of Kennedy's actions, the Russians were convinced that the United States would eventually start a war against Cuba, and their decision to deploy missiles there was partially motivated by the desire to deter an inevitable American invasion. Nixon could have persuaded the Russians that the United States had no plans for an invasion and that would have increased the chance to avoid the Cuban missile crisis. In all likelihood, the Russians would not have sent missiles to Cuba, accepting Nixon's guarantees not to invade the island.

THE MAIN QUESTION: VIETNAM

Historically, American presidents tend to make foreign-policy decisions that appear popular in the short run. National surveys taken since the 1940s also show America's overwhelming support for short-term military operations with a limited threat of casualties.[9] In 1965, the war in Vietnam appeared as a relatively short conflict and justifiable. The conflict was a reflection of a struggle against the destructive forces of communism, a chance to show America's strength to the world.[10] Therefore, supported by public opinion and being pushed by national security considerations, Nixon would have continued America's involvement in the Vietnam conflict and likely have escalated the war. This would have cost him the presidency in 1964 or at least would have diminished his chances for reelection. In this case, Senator Kennedy would have been again a strong and realistic choice for the Democratic Party.

Overall, Nixon, despite his strategic similarities with Kennedy, would have been a different president. Tactically, Nixon's actions, rooted in his ideological views and personality, would have altered the important details in the otherwise scripted course of the Cold War.

Conclusion

In a 1999 interview, former senator and presidential candidate Eugene McCarthy insisted that, in his view, Kennedy was a quintessential Cold War politician. Was Kennedy a hawk with an ideological commitment to the Cold War? Probably, he was. For a meticulous fact-finder,

Kennedy appears more in the mainstream of the Cold War presidency than an exceptional, innovative policymaker. He conducted an active foreign policy based on traditional foreign-policy foundations: a strong military, support of friendly nations, and interventionism. Kennedy's call for vigorous and innovative risks yielded to traditional policies that protected the global hegemony of the United States, thwarted Third World revolutions, and emphasized America's military superiority.[11]

In retrospect, Kennedy promised more than he was capable of delivering. He offered tax cuts. Yet, it was President Johnson who made these tax cuts proposals a real policy in 1964. Most of the 5 percent of the country's economic growth was due to massive military spending that boosted various sectors of the national economy. Kennedy did not appoint more women to top government positions compared to the previous administrations of Eisenhower and Truman. Kennedy was reluctant, due to political and electoral calculations, to move aggressively for the civil rights legislation. Sure, Johnson in 1964–65 was rewarded with a good measure of political fortune in domestic affairs. He had on his side a remarkably liberal Congress that passed some of the most far-reaching social legislation of the post-war era, including health care, federal aid to education, and civil rights.

However, despite setbacks, Kennedy's presidency reflected the inherent and renewed belief of many people in American exceptionalism and its global responsibility as a role model. Support for the leaders of newly independent African countries, the proposal for the Alliance for Progress in Latin America, the acceptance of an independent and neutral India, the Peace Corps and Food for Peace programs all reflected Washington's desire to enhance the American presence abroad. These dynamic policies reflected the president's personality and his image. Kennedy brought in a sense of excitement in many young people who perceived the Eisenhower era as "sleepy" years of inaction. Kennedy offered a vision of America that restored it to its historic position as the exemplary nation, a model for those countries that would aspire to liberty and wealth. Kennedy brought an inspiring vision to many people. Those hopes were cut short by his death. It is doubtful whether Nixon could have become a source of such inspiration had he been elected president in 1960.

— 5 —

1968: NIXON DEFEATS HUMPHREY—
LAW AND ORDER

1968: The Election Year

THE COUNTRY AND THE WORLD

If history had emotional bookmarks, the year of 1968 would be forever associated in people's collective memory with uncertainty, anxiety, and anticipation of change. It was the time of the student riots in Europe, the detonation of the youth counterculture, a massive international antiwar movement, and tragic assassinations of politicians. Conditions in Vietnam were worsening for the United States in 1968. The year began with the well-known Tet offensive and ended with the heaviest casualties since the beginning of the war: more than sixteen thousand American soldiers were killed. In August, the Soviet Union sent the armed forces of the Warsaw Pact to crush the reformist movement in Czechoslovakia. In Nigeria, one of the largest humanitarian disasters was developing around the self-proclaimed Republic of Biafra. In Greece, a NATO country, the military junta held its grip on power. An explosive situation continued in the Middle East. In April, Martin Luther King, Jr., was assassinated, and two months later, Senator Robert Kennedy was gunned down. The United States lost the USS *Scorpion*, an attack submarine carrying unidentified nuclear weapons in the Atlantic Ocean near the Azores, and at roughly the same time, tested its first hydrogen bomb.

BEFORE THE ELECTION

In 1968, primaries were not as integral to the nomination process as they have become now, because winning the primaries did not necessarily translate into delegates' votes. Most of the primaries were called "beauty contests"—the people were able to express their preferences but the delegate selection process was controlled by the state party organizations. Powerful political leaders, such as Mayor Richard J. Daley of Chicago, crowned nominees in the infamous smoke filled rooms.

It was commonly assumed in 1967 that President Johnson, elected in 1964 by a landslide, would be the Democratic nominee. Moreover, the best guess was that he would have little difficulty in winning the nomination. Only a few Democratic candidates at that time even contemplated running against a sitting president of his own party. One of the few was Senator Eugene J. McCarthy of Minnesota, who on November 30, 1967, announced his intention to run for the nomination of the Democratic Party. He started a nationwide campaign based on antiwar arguments and a promise for dramatic change in U.S. foreign policy. Scores of young people spread out in the primary states, knocking on doors and trumpeting his candidacy in what came to be known as the "Look Clean for Gene" campaign. He based his program on two themes: the first was change, a typical challenger's motto; the other was a message that he was an outsider to the Washington establishment.[1]

Twenty days in March 1968 dramatically altered the electoral situation in the Democratic Party. In the New Hampshire primaries on March 12, McCarthy showed surprisingly strong winning 42 percent of the primary vote compared to Johnson's 49 percent. More ominous for Johnson was the fact that McCarthy had received over five thousand write-in votes in the Republican primary. In light of the shifting balance, Senator Robert Kennedy of New York declared his candidacy four days later, on March 16. The next dramatic event came on March 31, when President Johnson announced, "I shall not seek and will not accept" the nomination from his party. This stunning decision left Senators Kennedy and McCarthy the two declared candidates for the Democratic presidential nomination. In April, however, Vice President Hubert Humphrey also joined the race. Although Kennedy was winning many votes in most state primaries and McCarthy was able to inspire millions of Americans,

Humphrey took the lead. Using his powerful connections as vice president and his long career as a leading liberal voice in American politics, he used the party establishment to become the clear frontrunner for the nomination. After Robert Kennedy's assassination in June, about half of his supporters went directly over to Humphrey. To complicate things further, by the time of the National Convention (August 26–29), Senator George S. McGovern also announced his candidacy. Things could not get more complicated.

Despite a seemingly unclear situation, Humphrey came to the 1968 Democratic National Convention in Chicago as a frontrunner with a surplus of potential delegates who would vote for him. He secured support from the black leaders, many labor groups, and most important, from the Democratic leaders of the South. During the convention, overcoming numerous procedural fights and challenges from McCarthy (Senator McCarthy for many years claimed that his challenges were dealt with unfairly), Humphrey won the nomination by more than a thousand votes, with the delegation from Pennsylvania putting him over the top. Humphrey chose Senator Edmund Muskie from Maine as his running mate.

In many ways it was a Pyrrhic victory, however. Humphrey's nomination was almost lost in the uproar surrounding the convention. Riots in the streets of Chicago and tear gas hanging over Grant Park upstaged the nomination. What the Walker Report was later to call "a police riot" was captured live on national television, something that the demonstrators were well aware of as they chanted, "the whole world is watching." Inside the convention center things were not much better. Supporters of the peace movement were threatening to hold a rump convention, and on national television from the floor of the convention, Senator Abraham Ribicoff denounced Mayor Daley and what he called the Gestapo tactics of the Chicago Police.

On the Republican side, Richard Nixon initially won a resounding victory in the important New Hampshire primary on March 12, winning 78 percent of the vote. Nixon had two challengers, both governors of big states. New York Governor Nelson Rockefeller defeated Nixon in the April 30 Massachusetts primary but could not capitalize on it and did poorly in other state primaries or conventions. Another opponent, California Governor Ronald Reagan, was California backed by many supporters from the conservative wing of the Republican Party, who remembered his stirring 1964 speech supporting Barry Goldwater. Reagan also ran against Nixon in primaries and even won California, but it was not enough to win the nomination. Nixon's nomination took place at the 1968 National Convention of the Republican Party in Miami Beach from August 5 to August 8. Nixon was nominated on the first ballot with 692 votes to 277 votes for Rockefeller, and 182 votes for Reagan.

After the Chicago Democratic Convention in late August, Humphrey trailed Nixon by double-digits in most polls, and his chances of winning in November seemed slim. September was a very bad month for Humphrey. He was taunted by antiwar protestors everywhere he went, and the party was so short of money that they could not buy enough airtime for him. Then at the end of September, Humphrey delivered his famous Salt Lake City speech in which he finally broke from the president on the war and announced his own plans to end it soon. By late October, Humphrey's clear statement on the war—in addition to the announcement about the possible halt of hostilities in Vietnam (nicknamed the "Halloween Peace")—gave him hope: the opinion polls showed that the final vote on November 5 would be very close.

The third-party candidate was Alabama Governor George Wallace running on populist and segregationist slogans. He appealed primarily to the middle and lower-middle class Americans disaffected with politics and ongoing liberal reforms. He also ran on an always-famous slogan of third-party candidates in the United States, saying that there was not a "dime's worth of difference" between Humphrey and Nixon. He, Wallace, told the electorate that he was the real candidate of difference.

RESULTS OF THE 1968 PRESIDENTIAL ELECTION

The winner of the 1968 presidential election (turnout was 60.6 percent) was named on Wednesday morning, November 6. Nixon won the popular vote with a plurality of just 512,000 votes, which was a victory margin of about one percentage point. In the Electoral College, Nixon's victory appeared larger, as he carried 32 states with 301 electoral votes, to Humphrey's 13 states and 191 electoral votes and Wallace's 5 states and 46 electoral votes. The three key states proved to be California, Ohio, and Illinois. Nixon won in these states by 3 percentage points or less, so that they provided 72 electoral votes to secure the victory. Humphrey received a majority of the vote in only 5 states: Minnesota (his home state), Maine (his running mate's home state), Massachusetts, Rhode Island, and Hawaii.

The third candidate, Governor Wallace, won almost ten million popular votes and carried five southern states: Alabama, Arkansas, Georgia, Louisiana, and Mississippi. If he had received more votes or if Nixon had lost either California or Ohio, for example, Wallace's showing would have thrown the election to the House of Representatives.

Nixon did well among high- and middle-income urban voters, who gave him a significant number of votes. For example, 54 percent of college graduates voted Republican, compared to 37 percent who voted Democratic (9 percent voted for Wallace). On the national scale, Nixon also did better among the rural population, taking 46 percent of the rural vote compared to 33 percent of the votes that went to Humphrey.[2] However, in the South, Governor Wallace took 41 percent of all rural votes, leaving both of his opponents with about 30 percent of the rural vote. Humphrey did significantly better among ethnic groups (only 5 percent of the black vote went to Nixon). Humphrey also received more than 6 percent of the vote in unionized neighborhoods. Yet, across the nation, two-thirds of people from low-income neighborhoods supported Humphrey. Nixon received 43 percent of men's votes and 41 percent of women's. Among women, 45 percent voted for Humphrey. According to 1968 Gallup final pre-election surveys, Nixon did better among independent and older voters. Twelve percent of the Democratic voters supported Nixon and 14 percent supported Wallace, which means that 26 percent of Democratic voters turned away from Humphrey. Nixon lost 14 percent of the Republican vote.

1968 Presidential Election
State-by-State Popular and Electoral College Vote

State	Hubert H. Humphrey (Democrat, MN)			Richard M. Nixon (Republican, CA)			George C. Wallace (American Ind., AL)		
	Vote	%	ECV	Vote	%	ECV	Vote	%	ECV
ALABAMA	195,918	18.8	-	146,591	14	-	687,664	65.8	10
ALASKA	35,411	42.7	-	37,600	45.3	3	10,024	12.1	-
ARIZONA	170,514	35	-	266,721	54.8	5	46,573	9.6	-
ARKANSAS	188,228	30.4	-	190,759	30.8	-	240,982	38.9	6
CALIFORNIA	3,244,318	44.7	-	3,467,664	47.8	40	487,270	6.7	-
COLORADO	335,174	41.3	-	409,345	50.5	6	60,813	7.5	-
CONNECTICUT	621,561	49.5	8	556,721	44.3	-	76,650	6.1	-
DELAWARE	89,194	41.6	-	96,714	45.1	3	28,459	13.3	-
D.C.	139,566	81.8	3	31,012	18.2	-	-	-	-
FLORIDA	676,794	30.9	-	886,405	40.5	14	624,207	28.5	-
GEORGIA	334,440	26.8	-	380,111	30.4	-	535,550	42.8	12
HAWAII	141,324	59.8	4	91,425	38.7	-	3,469	1.5	-
IDAHO	89,273	30.7	-	165,369	56.8	4	36,541	12.6	-
ILLINOIS	2,039,814	44.2	-	2,174,774	47.1	26	390,958	8.5	-
INDIANA	6,659	38	-	1,067,885	50.3	13	243,108	11.5	-
IOWA	476,699	40.8	-	619,106	53	9	66,422	5.7	-
KANSAS	302,996	34.7	-	478,674	54.8	7	88,921	10.2	-
KENTUCKY	397,541	37.7	-	462,411	43.8	9	193,098	18.3	-
LOUISIANA	309,615	28.2	-	309,615	28.2	-	530,300	48.3	10
MAINE	217,312	55.3	4	169,254	43.1	-	6,370	1.6	-
MARYLAND	538,310	43.6	10	517,995	41.9	-	178,734	14.5	-
MASSACHUSETTS	1,469,218	63	14	766,844	32.9	-	87,088	3.7	-

MICHIGAN	1,593,082	48.2	21	1,370,665	41.5	–	331,968	10	–
MINNESOTA	857,738	54	10	658,643	41.5	–	68,931	4.3	–
MISSISSIPPI	150,644	23	–	88,516	13.5	–	415,349	63.5	7
MISSOURI	791,444	43.7	–	811,932	44.9	12	206,126	11.4	–
MONTANA	114,117	41.6	–	138,835	50.6	4	20,015	7.3	–
NEBRASKA	170,784	31.8	–	321,163	59.8	5	44,904	8.4	–
NEVADA	60,598	39.3	–	73,188	47.5	3	20,432	13.3	–
NEW HAMPSHIRE	130,589	43.9	–	154,903	52.1	4	11,173	3.8	–
NEW JERSEY	1,264,206	44	–	1,325,467	46.1	17	262,187	9.1	–
NEW MEXICO	130,081	39.8	–	169,692	51.9	4	25,737	7.9	–
NEW YORK	3,378,470	49.8	43	3,007,932	44.3	–	358,864	5.3	–
N. CAROLINA	464,113	29.2	–	627,192	39.5	12	496,188	31.3	1
N. DAKOTA	94,769	38	–	138,669	55.9	4	14,244	5.8	–
OHIO	1,700,586	43	–	1,791,014	45.2	26	467,495	11.8	–
OKLAHOMA	301,658	32	–	449,697	47.7	8	191,731	20.3	–
OREGON	58,866	43.8	–	408,433	49.8	6	49,683	6.1	–
PENNSYLVANIA	2,259,403	47.6	29	2,090,017	44	–	378,582	8	–
RHODE ISLAND	246,518	64	4	122,359	31.8	–	15,678	4.1	–
S. CAROLINA	197,486	29.6	–	254,062	38.1	8	215,430	32.3	–
S. DAKOTA	118,023	42	–	149,841	53.3	4	13,400	4.8	–
TENNESSEE	351,233	28.1	–	472,592	37.9	11	424,792	34	–
TEXAS	1,266,804	41.1	25	1,227,844	39.9	–	584,269	19	–
UTAH	156,665	37.1	–	238,728	56.5	4	26,906	6.4	–
VERMONT	70,255	43.5	–	85,142	52.8	3	5,104	3.2	–
VIRGINIA	442,387	32.5	–	590,319	43.4	12	320,727	23.6	–
WASHINGTON	616,037	47.3	9	588,510	45.2	–	96,990	7.4	–
WEST VIRGINIA	374,091	49.6	7	307,555	0.8	–	72,560	9.6	–
WISCONSIN	748,804	44.3	–	809,997	47.9	12	127,835	7.6	–
WYOMING	45,173	35.5	–	70,927	55.8	3	11,105	8.7	–
	31,274,503	42.7	191	31,785,148	43.4	301	9,901,151	13.5	46

Source: http://psephos.adam-carr.net/countries/u/usa/pres/1968.txt

Nixon: How He Could Have Lost the 1968 Election

As we saw this tendency in the 1960 case, historically, in presidential elections, there is a direct correlation between presidential popularity in the year before the election and the outcome of the election even if the incumbent is not running for reelection. This means that low approval ratings of the sitting president are likely to have a serious negative impact on his party's chances. Average approval ratings of President Johnson throughout his presidency were at a respectable 55 percent, according to Gallup polls, yet in the spring of 1968, Johnson's approval ratings fell below 35 percent. The Vietnam War inspired mass protests. Violent reactions to Johnson's appearances were commonplace. The Secret Service limited his appearances across the country, especially near college towns. Johnson did not appear at the Democratic Convention in Chicago in August. However, it was not clear that Republicans and their candidate Richard Nixon would have had a clear advantage. A few things could have happened to contribute to a Nixon loss in November.

Democrats Appear Stronger

In 1968, the Democratic Party would have won against Nixon if it united and rallied behind one candidate. Internal disagreements and struggles led to a serious defeat of the party at the polls. History shows that a strong political party weakened by internal debates has a greater chance to lose the election altogether compared to a weaker party that comes (or appears to come) to the election unified. The most profound and notorious examples are the Russian Socialist Revolution in 1917 and Hitler's electoral takeover in Germany in 1933. In both cases, stronger but smaller parties were capable of outmaneuvering their bigger but disorganized opponents.

In 1968, the results of the election reflected more the Democratic Party's weakness than the Republican Party's strength. The thirty-plus-year-old Democratic coalition formed during the Roosevelt years was disintegrating. Opinion polls showed that 15 percent of blue-collar workers, traditionally supporting the party, were susceptible in the fall of 1968 to Wallace's populist and racist statements. Many liberal voters supporting McCarthy or Kennedy before the primaries were not enthusiastic about Vice President Humphrey and did not vote at all. The South was slowly swaying away from the Democratic Party. Conservative Democrats, many southerners, segregation supporters, and many who simply were disgusted with the youth counterculture turned to the Alabama governor George C. Wallace. Voting for Wallace was a sort of emotional catharsis for them, a response to frustration accumulated over time. The Democratic candidate received only 31 percent of the votes there, compared to 36 percent support for Nixon and 33 percent for Wallace. There was no clear leadership or a solid plan to consolidate the party and its strategic platform in 1968. A party nominating its strongest leader has a very good chance to win the November election, while a party nominating just a fine person risks defeat in November.[3]

Humphrey and his supporters believed that the best alternative to costly debates would be a continuation of the previous course of the Johnson administration but with some healthy corrections. Humphrey supporters also believed that once the nation extricated itself from Vietnam, the situation would dramatically improve and strengthen their leadership position in the party. Humphrey received strong support from the Democratic Party establishment, which was controlled by labor union leaders and politicians representing large cities. Unfortunately, this support was not enough to help him secure a victory in November.

JOHNSON STAYS IN THE RACE

What if President Johnson had stayed in the race as the expected candidate or retracted his earlier statement and reentered? Several factors motivated Johnson's decision to drop out of the contest. First, he faced a seemingly difficult political campaign ahead due to serious challengers within the party, especially from Senator McCarthy. Second, there were also, as he claimed, continuous stress, fatigue, and overall poor health. One of the recent polls that he saw showed that support for the war in Vietnam had fallen to 26 percent—one of the lowest levels ever. He justified his decision by the desire to eliminate politics from the presidential race and in the name of national unity. In fact, he accomplished just the opposite.

If Johnson stayed in the race as an incumbent, the outcome of the 1968 election could have been different. Despite McCarthy supporters' claims that they could have won the party nomination and the election because of their clear success during the New Hampshire primaries, most likely Johnson could have secured the nomination. His party would have been less divided and the opinions within the party would have been less polarized. As the incumbent, Johnson could have raised more money for the Democratic Party to stay competitive in close races against Nixon.

McCarthy Does Not Run

Senator McCarthy led a significant opposition group within the party for almost a year. Considerably less organized than the pro-establishment groups, this faction brought together various groups of people who were younger than the average Democratic voter, dissatisfied with the status quo, and strongly opposed to the war in Vietnam. Although McCarthy, in his own words, believed that he represented the typical Democratic voter who was generally conservative about domestic issues and relatively hawkish against foreign threats, his supporters were far more liberal and distinctively anti-establishment than the average voter.

McCarthy could have chosen to stay out of the race. Why did he decide to run for the White House? According to his own recollection, several reasons motivated his decision. First, it was his disappointment about the administration's incompetence in executing the war, especially with Secretary of State Rusk and Secretary of Defense McNamara. Second, he mentioned his deep disappointment with the entire political climate in the Senate. He was unable to launch a serious discussion about the war on the Senate floor. The third reason was Lyndon Johnson's arrogance: Johnson frequently accused the war opponents, and one of them was McCarthy himself, of being cowards. If the opponents of the war received more opportunity to influence U.S. policies in Vietnam, or if the administration was able to show competence in handling the war and the political situation around it, the likelihood of an effective challenge from McCarthy and within the party would have diminished.

ROBERT KENNEDY DOES NOT JOIN THE RACE

Robert Kennedy brought both hope and confusion to the Democratic campaign. He, like McCarthy, also ran his campaign based on a slogan: "The country wants to move in a different direction." Although being very critical of the war, Kennedy was not a clear antiwar candidate (it was his brother, JFK, in fact, who had first committed U.S. troops to the war in Vietnam). He was, however, capable of unifying many black and minority voters, a substantial chunk of Catholic voters, and those who still sympathized with JFK, assassinated in 1963.

There is a general disagreement about whether or not Robert Kennedy had a real chance to win the nomination. It is a myth that he was a clear frontrunner after winning California primaries. When he was assassinated in early June, he already trailed Humphrey in terms of delegate votes, having secured 393 votes compared to 561 votes pledged to Humphrey. McCarthy, who secured 258 votes by that time, maintained for a long time that Kennedy, in fact, had caused havoc and uncertainty. McCarthy claimed that Kennedy had split the party into several factions, which eventually influenced the outcome of the general election. McCarthy supporters were united in their claims that Kennedy made a selfish move when he entered the race after the New Hampshire primaries. McCarthy also believed that he did most of the hard work during the winter, persuading the voters to rethink the war and challenge the administration. In a way, Kennedy's candidacy divided the antiwar movement and took away votes from the McCarthy camp.

WALLACE WINS ENOUGH VOTES

Wallace could have taken the election of the new president to the House of Representatives if no candidate secured 270 electoral votes. This would have brought the victory to the Democratic candidate. Wallace was supposed to win over many of the conservative voters. About two-thirds of his supporters, in theory, could have voted for Nixon. Wallace could have split the conservative vote, especially in the South. However, at the same time, Wallace took enough votes from Humphrey; for example, Wallace took about 15 percent of the overall union votes in November.

Overall, Wallace's inability to take too many votes from Nixon was a factor contributing to the Republican Party candidate's success. In particular, Wallace could have done slightly better in just three states to send the election to the House. In Florida, he needed approximately 130,000 extra votes to win the state (out of about 2 million votes cast). In North Carolina, he needed approximately 60,000 votes (in addition to the 496,000 votes he received). In South Carolina, he needed an additional 20,000 votes on top of his 215,000 to have changed history. In the context of the calculations the assumption is that all of these "additional votes" should have come at the expense of Nixon.

ROMNEY AND REAGAN SERIOUSLY CHALLENGE NIXON

Nixon did not face tough competition within the Republican Party. Although George Romney, governor of Michigan, announced his intention to run for the Republican nomination, he was quickly out of the race in February 1968. He served later in the first Nixon administration as the secretary of housing and urban development. Reagan also could have posed a more serious challenge to Nixon. However, this probability remained insignificant. In fact, the Republicans did not have an issue that could have seriously divided their ranks. They faced opponents who were divided, which helped them maintain the perception of unity. In addition, Nixon was an experienced campaigner who was able to preserve substantial support in the country from his years in the Eisenhower administration.

NIXON DOES NOT STAY ON MESSAGE

The 1968 Republican Party platform was rooted in cautious promises of stability. It was the "law and order" campaign, and a thinly disguised attack on the Warren Court, which was portrayed as too liberal and soft on crime. Although critics maintained that such a slogan is more applicable for a sheriff running for a local office than to a presidential candidate, many people liked it anyway. Nixon never promised peace in Vietnam "at any price" as many Democrats demanded. At his Republican Convention acceptance speech, Nixon promised only to "bring an honorable end to the war in Vietnam." He called for the strengthening of the national defense and lower taxes. Nixon asked people to stop "screaming" at each other and to start a dialogue. The Republican Party was able to develop an appropriate social agenda, which appeared as more important than the economic agenda championed by the Democrats. Nixon was able to appeal to the center of the electorate.[4] Moreover, Nixon developed a strategy designed to appeal to conservative, white southerners. Traditionally Democratic, many of them were disaffected by Johnson and Humphrey's support for the civil rights movement.

The radical antiwar movement shared the fate of similar popular protest movements from other countries. While granting the movement some initial successes, the conduct of the youthful radicals repelled many potential antiwar members of the middle class. As far as this argument goes, the radical antiwar movement ultimately had little effect on the conduct of the war. Even worse, it may actually have prolonged the war because it gave the opposition powerful arguments why the war was necessary.[5]

John Ehrlichman, one of Nixon's campaign advisers, summarized two main messages that helped Nixon win the 1968 election. Both messages emphasized the *immaturity* of the opponents and stability and *maturity* of his presidential platform. Specifically, Nixon maintained that the Democratic opponents were deeply divided. Moreover, the Democratic Party had been taken over by the "fringe elements" and "a bunch of loonies" who could not be trusted. Nixon sustained the message that he and his party still had a sense of direction in an unstable world, and that he would not let the Russians or the Chinese "push us around."[6]

In retrospect, Nixon was able to persuade many voters that Humphrey's platform was turning to the left from the traditional democratic course. This contributed to Wallace's success in the South and ultimately cost the Democratic Party the election. Moreover, Nixon was able to attract many votes in the South thus launching the so-called southern strategy for the Republican Party in the 1968 election. After that year, the Republicans won five of eight presidential elections between 1968 and 1996, largely because their candidates were able to win in the South. Significantly, the only Democrats able to capture the White House during the following three decades were southerners—Jimmy Carter in 1976, and Bill Clinton in 1992 and 1996.[7]

THE "HALLOWEEN PEACE" WORKED

Johnson had a very ambivalent position about the war in Vietnam. As Jack Valenti, his aide, said, "Johnson's sole motivation was to try, as we say in Texas, 'To haul ass out of that war,' get out of there. He didn't know how to do it."[8] One of the reasons for Johnson's reluctance to end the war was political. He did not want to appear weak and give the Republicans the moral ammunition to accuse him of losing the Cold War. The Vietnam War ended the foreign-policy consensus in the United States. There was a general agreement among the American public since the 1930s over the course of the country's foreign policy. The first major challenge to the "consensus" was at the end of the Korean War back in the 1950s. Gallup polls in 1967 showed that just 30 percent of Americans were opposed to the war in Vietnam. The opposition grew rapidly in 1968, after the bloody Tet offensive when more than half of the American people opposed the war.

A promise of a quick ending of the war in Vietnam would have improved Humphrey's position as a candidate. Any progress reported by South Vietnamese President Nguyen Van Thieu regarding the peace talks would also have helped the Democrats and Humphrey. A possibility for him suddenly opened on October 31, when President Johnson announced a complete cessation of "all air, naval, and artillery bombardment of North Vietnam" effective the next day. It appeared that Johnson believed that he could halt the war before the election in November, which would have given Humphrey, as a candidate, extra votes. Earlier in October, Humphrey himself was talking about a bombing halt. Opinion polls showed the gap between him and Nixon closing, although it is difficult to attribute these results to the course of the war alone.

If Nixon Were Not Elected

Just imagine that Nixon had lost in 1968. After Nixon's second defeat in presidential elections in eight years, newspapers across America might have commented about the 1968 Humphrey victory: *The search for a just and durable peace has been the keystone of Hubert Humphrey's campaign. He was the right candidate to move America forward. The challenge was urgent, the task was large, the time was now.* Republicans would have assumed that Nixon's message was weak, that he did not have the necessary charisma to be a president, and that young voters were uninspired by his candidacy. Democrats would have forgotten about last year's disagreements and united behind president-elect Humphrey. Next, the attention would have switched to Humphrey's cabinet nominations.

Expectedly, there was a wide range of speculation about Humphrey's prospective White House cabinet. Many from the Johnson administration would have liked to continue. However, Senator Walter Mondale, who occupied Humphrey's former Senate seat from Minnesota and was co-chairman of Humphrey's campaign committee, argued that Humphrey needed to distance himself from President Johnson.[9] The name of Chicago mayor Richard Daley was circulating in the press as a possible top cabinet member. Back in the summer of 1968, after the Democratic convention, some advisers suggested that Humphrey ask Ted Kennedy to join him as his running mate. One of the advantages of such an option could have been to retain the backing of Robert Kennedy's supporters. Humphrey considered this idea but never accepted it. He thought most Kennedy supporters would have voted for him anyway. Rumors in the mainstream press also suggested in late October that Humphrey, if elected, might create two additional cabinet posts—one dealing with youth, the other with consumer issues.[10] The name of Clark Clifford was hinted as a candidate for secretary of defense (he was appointed to this post by Johnson early in 1968). The post of secretary of state could go to George Ball or McGeorge Bundy. Robert McNamara and Cleveland

Mayor Carl Stokes were mentioned interchangeably for the Departments of Transportation and of Housing and Urban Development. A Humphrey cabinet would have included some moderate Republicans, such as Nelson Rockefeller. Patricia Roberts Harris, former Ambassador to Luxembourg, could have become the secretary of the Department of Health, Education, and Welfare (she was appointed to this position by President Carter in 1977).

THE HUMPHREY DOCTRINE?

Pragmatism became a cornerstone of Nixon's foreign policy. What was later labeled as the "Nixon doctrine" was a set of at least three principles or imperatives in foreign policy. First, the United States should keep all of its treaty commitments with other countries. Second, Washington should provide a shield to any allied nation or any country whose survival is vital to U.S. security. Third, in cases of direct aggression, the United States would furnish military and economic assistance when requested by a sovereign nation. However, Washington expected this nation to assume the primary responsibility of providing for its defense. Nixon wanted to reduce American military involvement overseas. Once in office, Nixon proposed a Vietnam strategy of replacing American troops with Vietnamese troops, a move that, in his view, did not look like surrender.

If Humphrey were president, what would have been his foreign policy doctrine? He would have certainly inherited from the Johnson administration a long-term policy of supporting governments "friendly" to the United States. He would have had little problem of justifying such policies based on security concerns. However, if he attempted a unilateral and immediate withdrawal from Vietnam, he would have met serious opposition not only from the Republicans but also from his own party. Out of security concerns, many of his critics would have argued that the United States would weaken its own position in Asia and strengthen the status of the Soviet Union and China in the region. From a political standpoint, unilateral concessions would have created vulnerability for the Democrats in the 1970 midterm elections as well as the presidential election in 1972. Such concessions would have given the Republican Party ammunition to portray Humphrey and the Democrats as weak on foreign policy. One of the advantages of Nixon's position was that, as a hardliner, he would have taken reconciliatory steps toward both communist adversaries without appearing vulnerable and weak. Confidence and strength—often a subjective factor based on perception—give a politician significant flexibility.

Humphrey eventually would have accepted a strategy based on the assumption that the Cold War tensions were actually necessary for world stability, and that both the Soviet Union and the United States have legitimate strategic interests and "zones of influence." Like Nixon, Humphrey should have accepted the view that the nuclear arsenals of the Soviet Union and the United States were, in general terms, equal. Therefore, to guarantee peace, both governments should have used the doctrine of "Mutual Assured Destruction" as the foundation of their nuclear policies. This strategy was adopted when Robert McNamara was serving as secretary of defense. It was based on the assumption that both countries had accumulated enough nuclear power to destroy each other. Therefore, the combined nuclear arsenals of the United States and the Soviet Union served as a major mutual deterrent. It would have been suicidal for either country to launch a nuclear war against the other.

An Exit from Vietnam

John F. Kennedy and Lyndon Johnson believed that being in Vietnam was the price that their generation had to bear in the Cold War. For Kennedy, the war in Vietnam was a moral crusade. However, the White House leadership did not understand Vietnamese culture and the power of the combination of communist ideology and nationalism. Despite all the honorable intentions, the communists' willingness to sacrifice was far stronger than the American desire to "pay any price" to defend freedom, as Kennedy proclaimed back in 1960. When Nixon took office, more than half a million American soldiers were deployed in Vietnam. By the end of 1972 there were about 330,000, and by 1974 there were less than 25,000.

Humphrey, as president, could have tried to end the war before the election year of 1972 and on America's terms. He could have done this, as Nixon did, through rapprochement with China and the Soviet Union and in some form of a settlement with North Vietnam. In the process, Humphrey would likely have stayed away from an escalation of the war in Laos and Cambodia. Despite Nixon's efforts, the Soviet Union and North Vietnam did not want to negotiate. They both considered the war as an anti-colonial showdown and believed that history was on the Vietnamese side. (The 1973 peace accords did not actually stop the fighting.) Nixon was able to connect the exit from Vietnam with an improvement of relations with China and the Soviet Union. Nixon understood the principle of the domino effect. He too did not want to lose Vietnam and Southeast Asia to communist expansionism. Yet Nixon was able to find a compromise and eventually to bargain with the Soviets and Chinese. Nixon chose the best among all the worse options available in Vietnam. Humphrey would not have approved such a strategy.

HUMPHREY AND THE SOVIET UNION

Nixon and his secretary of state, Henry Kissinger, are credited among others for the policy of détente, or a general reduction of tensions between Washington and Moscow. Nixon used the improving international environment to address the issue of nuclear peace, a term used during the Cold War to describe nuclear stability guaranteed by key nuclear powers. Humphrey would have supported the ongoing negotiations to limit the two countries' stockpiles of atomic weapons. Most probably, the Strategic Arms Limitation Talks would have ended with a treaty. Similarly, the Anti-Ballistic Missile Treaty and an agreement about limitating strategic offensive arms would have been completed. This would certainly have helped improve relations between the United States the Soviet Union. It is less likely, however, that Humphrey would have been in a good position to pursue the policy of maintaining active dialogue and frequent summits with the Soviet leadership. Being aware of the possible accusations from the Republicans, Humphrey would have to have demonstrated strength in dealing with the Soviets, and would thus have displayed a cautious attitude toward the leaders behind the Kremlin's walls. If the United States exited from Vietnam, the Soviet Union would have considered this a moral victory for its own policies, and would have continued to apply pressure and challenge Washington in many regions, including Africa and Asia. This, in turn, would have caused a harsh reaction from the United States. Trying to compensate for the defeat in Vietnam, the Humphrey administration would have needed to continue to demonstrate strength in other regions. Tensions between the Soviet Union and America would have continued to escalate.

No Rapprochement with China

The tension between the Soviet Union and China, two communist nations, reached its peak by the end of the 1960s. Nixon decided to use their bitter conflict to shift the balance of power in the course of the Cold War. It was necessary for several reasons, including the need to settle the conflict in Vietnam and to weaken the position of the Soviet Union. Despite his profound ideological distaste of communism, he decided to approach the Chinese Communist government and start a dialogue. Top Chinese leadership was convinced that American imperialism would eventually fall; yet it also believed that a temporary improvement of relations between the two nations would be beneficial to China. Both countries also knew that any improvement in mutual relations between them would alarm the Soviet Union. As a result, Moscow began to pursue its own policy of reconciliation with the United States in the name of international security.

Humphrey would not likely have pursued the new approach in the U.S. policy toward China. If he had decided to end the war in Vietnam unilaterally, he would not have needed better relations with China. Nor would he have seen at that time any strategic necessity to develop friendly relations with China despite the evidence of the growing conflict between Peking and Moscow. As a liberal politician, he also would have faced serious opposition at home that would have accused him of accommodating China and its leadership. Humphrey would not have wanted to give his political opponents additional ammunition to criticize his foreign policies. Nixon's policies toward China were conducted initially in the atmosphere of secrecy and deception, which obviously helped Nixon avoid criticism and opposition. Humphrey's policies would have been more transparent and therefore more vulnerable to disapproval and challenge right from the beginning.

THE MIDDLE EAST

During Nixon's White House days, the United States had produced a significant shift of the power balance in the Middle East. The prime objective of U.S. policy was to weaken the Soviet influence in the region. First, from a Cold War ally, Israel had become a strategic asset in the Middle East. The rapid transition began after the Six Day War in 1967. Humphrey as president would have accepted this changing role of Israel and supported pro-Israeli policies. Also, in 1967 American public opinion was largely supportive of Israel, which would have been a factor in Humphrey's policies.

DOMESTIC POLICIES: NOMINATION RULES

After winning the White House in 1968, Humphrey would have pushed for a reform in the nomination process for the next presidential election. As a probable candidate in 1972, he would have wanted to eliminate the turmoil of the nomination process that marked the infamous election year of 1968. After the chaotic 1968 convention in Chicago, most top Democrats urged serious action to prevent such a disaster from happening again. As a result, a special commission (known as the McGovern-Fraser Commission) was convened to reexamine the manner in which delegates were chosen. The commission made recommendations to change the nomination process to make it more open. The Republicans also designed a similar review group. Based on these political moves, the role of national conventions was dramatically diminished after 1968. This has also meant a relative weakening of the power of party insiders in the nomination process.

Ordinary voters began to play an increasingly important role in the nomination process. McCarthy's unsuccessful run actually helped other candidates considered "outsiders" to gain prominence during the primaries. For example, the new rules clearly played a significant role in the nomination of Governor Jimmy Carter in 1976. Factors such as prominence of a candidate or a candidate's visibility on the national scene became crucial in the selection of candidates. The focus was shifting to the candidate's image. This has certainly given special status to early primaries and state caucuses in states such as Iowa, New Hampshire, South Carolina, and Florida. An early primary win provides tremendous media attention and guaranteed name recognition in the near term, possibly resulting in additional votes received by a candidate. The 1968 debacle in the Democratic Party was a significant factor that caused changes in the nomination process resulting in more power for governors and state legislatures. Remarkably, during a thirty-year period after 1976, four out of five presidents were former governors.

Humphrey as president most probably would have been able to consolidate the Democratic Party, which experienced an internal turmoil in the late 1960s. Two major issues, the war in Vietnam and civil rights reforms, had separated the party into several factions. Following a Humphrey victory, many southern Democrats would likely have stayed with the party and voted for its candidates for years to come. Humphrey's attempts to end the war soon would have also accommodated some antiwar activists. He would also have witnessed the process of the "institutionalization of radicalism," a social process of implementing formerly radical ideas (or the ideas that appeared radical) into societal institutional policies and structures. In fact, his proposal to create a special federal agency dealing with youth could have been an attempt to find a compromise between young people's ideas and institutional policies.

There is insufficient evidence to suggest that Humphrey would have initiated certain policies that Nixon took credit for. As president, Humphrey, like Nixon, would have imposed wage and price controls, indexed Social Security for inflation, and created Supplemental Security Income. He also would have created institutions similar to the Environmental Protection Agency, Occupational Safety and Health Administration, the

National Oceanic and Atmospheric Administration, the National Railroad Passenger Corporation, the Drug Enforcement Administration, and the Office of Minority Business Enterprise. Most probably, Humphrey would not have reorganized the Post Office Department (Nixon created a new government-owned corporation, the U.S. Postal Service). Humphrey would have also attempted to establish several federal affirmative action programs, and would have increased salaries for federal employees. Desegregation of schools would have also been a Humphrey achievement. He also, as Nixon did, would have signed a bill that lowered the maximum U.S. speed limit to fifty-five miles per hour.

Unlike Nixon, Humphrey might have continued with ambitious space exploration plans. He would have endorsed the establishment of a permanent base on the moon by the end of the 1970s and the launch of a manned expedition to Mars in the early 1980s. Humphrey, like Nixon, would have tried healthcare reform, which would have taken the form of a universal healthcare plan. Facing increasing oil prices, Humphrey would have certainly established some government controls of production, marketing, and distribution of oil in the United States.

If Humphrey became president, the U.S. Supreme Court would not have had Warren E. Burger (Chief Justice), Harry Andrew Blackmun, Lewis Franklin Powell Jr., and William Rehnquist (Chief Justice in 1986). Antonin Scalia would have been appointed to Rehnquist's seat as an associate justice. The two most visible aspects of Rehnquist's tenure as Chief Justice were his presiding over the impeachment trial of Bill Clinton and the *Bush v. Gore* decision.

WATERGATE IS JUST AN APARTMENT COMPLEX IN D.C.

Nixon's name is prominently associated with the Watergate scandal, one of the most remarkable and infamous events in the history of the presidency in the twentieth century. Without Nixon as president, this event would not have happened. After Watergate, Congress made several decisions to limit the power of the presidency. The War Powers Resolution of 1973, for example, allows the president to use military forces for sixty days, without a formal declaration of war by Congress.

Additionally, without Watergate, politics would have remained an attractive career choice for more young people. If Watergate never happened, most of us would have been less cynical about Washington and the White House. It also would have taken a longer time for investigative journalism to reach its current strength.

When Nixon resigned, the Soviet leaders were in a state of disbelief. They could not imagine that such a powerful world leader could not restrain some noisy legislators and the press. The Watergate scandal raised the suspicions of the Soviet leaders who were convinced that what happened to Nixon was a "payback" for his friendly relations with the Soviet Union and his contribution to détente.

Watergate dealt a mortal blow to Nixon's attempt at long-term voting realignment. Many conservative Democratic states turned back to the Democratic Party, which appeared less corrupt and more transparent than its opponents were. Many people who voted for Nixon in 1968 became swing voters after Watergate, thus bringing Carter to the White House in 1976.

Conclusion

The growth of conservative attitudes was a crucial factor allowing Nixon to win in 1968. His narrow electoral victory changed the United States and the world. Nixon surfed on the wave of growing American conservatism. There are two types of conservative views. The first one is *ideological*. It is based on deeply seated conservative principles and values, most likely coming from a person's early experiences. The other type of conservative view is called *responsive*. It is commonly rooted in a person's dissatisfaction with ongoing or anticipated changes. To reduce this state of anxiety or disappointment and to return to a more familiar and friendly worldview, the individual turns to so-called traditional values based on stability, order, and predictability. History shows that across the world, attempts at rapid social change commonly cause a conservative backlash.

One of the most serious causes of responsive conservatism is people's fear about the lack of stability. To many Americans during this period, a new generation had suddenly grown up. They appeared disinterested in the "normal" issues that had preoccupied older generations. They wore different clothes, spoke a different language, and smoked marijuana. This stereotypical and negative image of the "hippie generation" caused anxiety among many people. The antiwar movement of the 1960s, the riots in several large American cities, the appearance of the new youth counterculture, and the resulting feelings of insecurity, altogether contributed to this sense of anxiety and the desire to return to stability. This is a typical human reaction. Conservatism is also a no-confidence vote to politicians associated with instability. From 1964 to 1970, the percentage of Americans who considered themselves conservative had jumped from 28 to 41 percent, and the number of people referring to themselves as liberal went down from 26 to 22 percent.[11] Voters tend to respond to salient issues rather than to conceptually difficult ones.[12] Any salient issue may become crucial for retrospective evaluations. The election of Nixon, in fact, was a self-justification of many people's conservative attitudes: this was their conservative response to changes that they did not welcome.

Nixon was very successful in promoting the concept of the "silent majority," saying that there are other people and interests other than demonstrating, rioting, doing drugs, and being a hippie. Nixon was able to attract people, including the southerners, ethnic minorities, Catholics, and members of labor unions, who were disappointed with the radical changes.[13] Nixon was representing a fight, as his supporters would say, against "amnesty, abortion, and acid." Most people rejected the idea of the social revolution. Many people thought Nixon was on the other side of the barricades defending order against "revolutionaries." The alleged destruction of the merit system coming with the advancement of feminism and multiculturalism, court-ordered quotas to desegregate schools, and the busing of children were seen by many as an attempt to change American social fabric. Rapid changes in the social sphere, such as birth clinics and tolerance toward open sexuality, were also frightening to many. Mandatory restrictions including gun control, ignition-controlled seat belts, or bans on all-male choirs looked ridiculous to many ordinary Americans. All of this had serious electoral consequences for the Democratic Party. Television and newspaper reports about violence on the streets discouraged many to give support to the antiwar movement.

Unlike Kennedy, Nixon never became a source of admiration. History retains his public image as a loner, preoccupied with his own insecurities and fear, a person overwhelmed with his personal vendetta against his enemies, a lonely and quiet insider with few close friends. Historians emphasize Nixon's uneasiness and even unhappiness dealing with domestic problems during his tenure in politics. He seemed to be passionate only about campaigning and foreign policy. But even in foreign policy, the best deals came out of secret negotiations and missions he planned and conducted for many months, hidden from public eyes.

Nixon carried on his shoulders a conservative wave that made its way back to public life. Without a backlash against Nixon, Reagan's rise to power would probably not have taken place. Nixon ended the war in Vietnam. In the process, he brought China back to the negotiating table. His détente with the Soviets made them accept the status quo, and thus stopped their ambitious charge toward what they hoped would be global domination.

In his *Six Crises* book published in 1962, Nixon described the most crucial moments of his political career—the moments of crises—that brought him prominence and experience and altogether propelled him to the White House in 1968. One of his main convictions was that without losing, a person could never fulfill himself. "Only in losing himself does he find himself."[14]

— 6 —

2000: BUSH DEFEATS GORE— THE COURT DECIDES

2000: The Election Year

THE COUNTRY AND THE WORLD

The world had just finished celebrating a new millennium. The dot-com boom continued and the corporate world witnessed its largest merger as Time-Warner bought America Online. Russia elected a new president, Vladimir Putin, Venezuela reelected Hugo Chavez, and crude oil prices were around $30 per barrel. India's population had reached one billion and the United States approached 293 million inhabitants. Israel withdrew its forces from southern Lebanon after being there for more than two decades and Yugoslavia's strong man, Milosevic, resigned. Bill Clinton visited Vietnam, and his wife, Hillary, was elected to the United States Senate.

BEFORE THE ELECTION

As the vice president to the only Democratic president to win two full terms of office since Franklin Roosevelt, Al Gore was well positioned to win the Democratic Party's nomination for the presidency in 2000. Early on several prominent Democrats tested the waters. Nebraska Senator Bob Kerrey, Missouri Congressman Dick Gephardt, and Minnesota Senator Paul Wellstone were mentioned as possible candidates, but in the end, none of them chose to seek the nomination. Only Senator Bill Bradley of New Jersey entered the competition.

Bradley characterized Gore as a conservative; Gore and President Clinton were both members of the centrist Democratic Leadership

133

Council. Bradley's attack on the centrist positions of Gore and Clinton was an attempt to build a political coalition to the left of Gore. Essentially, Bradley followed an insurgent's strategy to obtain maximum attention and name recognition, but he was never able to carry it far. After losing in the Iowa caucuses, Bradley managed to poll almost 46 percent of the vote in New Hampshire. Although a respectable showing, it still amounted to a second place finish behind Gore. More important, New Hampshire was Bradley's best outing. Although he struggled on through much of March, Bradley eventually withdrew his candidacy, leaving Gore without a serious challenger.

When the Democrats, meeting in Los Angeles late in August, arrived at the business of selecting their nominee the choice was not only a foregone conclusion but also a unanimous one. Since Bradley had withdrawn, his name was not even put before the convention. The only remaining issue was the nomination of the vice presidential candidate. Here, Gore chose Senator Joseph Lieberman of Connecticut. Lieberman was the first Democratic senator to publicly criticize President Clinton over the Monica Lewinsky scandal, and his selection was generally seen as an attempt by Gore to distance himself from Clinton.

Initially, the Republicans had a wealth of serious candidates. The clear frontrunner, however, was George W. Bush, son of the former President George H.W. Bush. The son's family connections, obvious name recognition, and his experience as the governor of Texas attracted early support from the Republican establishment. Unlike his father, George W. Bush had also cultivated support from Christian conservative activists who had never quite trusted the senior Bush. As the frontrunner, Governor Bush was able to quickly build a campaign fund that easily outstripped most of his opponents. The only candidate who could match him in spending was Steve Forbes. After failing to secure his nomination in 1996, Forbes put up only token opposition in 2000.

As the primaries approached, it became apparent that the race for the nomination was between Governor Bush and Arizona Senator John McCain. Early on McCain looked like a formidable challenger. A former POW in Vietnam with a reputation for being an outspoken maverick in the Senate, McCain appealed to many moderate Republicans and Independents. Still it was somewhat of a surprise when he beat Governor Bush in New Hampshire. Suddenly he looked like a very serious challenge to the frontrunner. However, after a hard fought and nasty campaign in South Carolina, McCain's chances began to dim. Although he did go on to win other primary contests, his campaign never recovered from the loss in South Carolina.

In the end, Governor Bush carried the Republican convention with 2,038 of 2,041 delegate votes. Anticipating his victory, Governor Bush had asked former Secretary of Defense Richard (Dick) Cheney to head an exploratory committee to select a running mate. In the end, the governor chose Cheney himself. With Governor Bush's recommendation, Cheney was nominated by a voice vote of the convention.

Third parties also nominated two other candidates of note in 2000. Pat Buchanan, after flirting with seeking the Republican nomination, was selected by the Reform Party. Additionally, the Green Party selected Ralph Nader as its standard bearer.

RESULTS OF THE 2000 ELECTION

Against the backdrop of peace and economic growth, the expectation was that Gore would defeat his rival and extend the Democrat's hold on the presidency another four years. Expectations to the contrary, the election returns constituted an extremely close vote total. Both candidates carried about 48 percent of the popular vote.

Even as the votes were being cast and counted, the television networks were busily making predictions. It soon became clear that the election would be decided by Florida and its Electoral College votes. At about 8:00 p.m., the networks placed Florida in the Gore column and declared him the winner. But two hours later they backed off of their projection and placed Florida in the undecided column, leaving the election results unsettled. Finally, early the next morning, the networks, with about 15 percent of the Florida votes still uncounted, declared Bush the winner of Florida and thus the election. The problem was that most of those uncounted votes were in heavily Democratic areas of the state.

2000 Presidential Election
State-by-State Popular and Electoral College Vote

State	George W. Bush (Republican, TX)			Albert A. Gore (Democrat, TN)			Ralph Nader (Green Party, CT)	
	Vote	%	ECV	Vote	%	ECV	Vote	ECV
ALABAMA	941,173	56.47	9	692,611	41.59	–	18,323	–
ALASKA	167,398	58.62	3	79,004	27.67	–	28,747	–
ARIZONA	781,652	50.95	8	685,341	44.67	–	45,645	–
ARKANSAS	472,940	51.31	6	422,768	45.86	–	13,421	–
CALIFORNIA	4,567,429	41.65	–	5,861,203	53.45	54	418,707	–
COLORADO	883,748	50.75	8	738,227	42.39	–	91,434	–
CONNECTICUT	561,094	38.44	–	816,015	55.9	8	64,452	–
DELAWARE	137,288	41.9	–	180,068	54.96	3	8,307	–
D.C.	18,073	8.95	–	171,923	85.16	2	10,576	–
FLORIDA	2,912,790	48.85	25	2,912,253	48.84	–	97,488	–
GEORGIA	1,419,720	54.67	13	1,116,230	42.98	–	*13,432	–
HAWAII	137,845	37.46	–	205,286	55.79	4	21,623	–
IDAHO	336,937	67.17	4	138,637	27.64	–	*12,292	–
ILLINOIS	2,019,421	42.58	–	2,589,026	54.6	22	103,759	–
INDIANA	1,245,836	56.65	12	901,980	41.01	–	*18,531	–
IOWA	634,373	48.22	–	638,517	48.54	7	29,374	–
KANSAS	622,332	58.04	6	399,276	37.24	–	36,086	–
KENTUCKY	872,492	56.5	8	638,898	41.37	–	23,192	–
LOUISIANA	927,871	52.55	9	792,344	44.88	–	20,473	–
MAINE	286,616	43.97	–	319,951	49.09	4	37,127	–
MARYLAND	813,797	40.18	–	1,145,782	56.57	10	53,768	–
MASSACHUSETTS	878,502	32.5	–	1,616,487	59.8	12	173,564	–

State	Votes	%	EV	Votes	%	EV	Votes	EV
MICHIGAN	1,953,139	46.28	-	2,170,418	51.28	18	84,165	-
MINNESOTA	1,109,659	45.5	-	1,168,266	47.91	10	126,696	-
MISSISSIPPI	572,844	57.62	7	404,614	40.7	-	8,122	-
MISSOURI	1,189,924	50.42	11	1,111,138	47.08	-	38,515	-
MONTANA	240,178	58.44	3	137,126	33.36	-	24,437	-
NEBRASKA	433,862	62.25	5	231,780	33.25	-	24,540	-
NEVADA	301,575	49.52	4	279,978	45.98	-	15,008	-
NEW HAMPSHIRE	273,559	48.07	4	266,348	46.8	-	22,198	-
NEW JERSEY	1,284,173	40.29	-	1,788,850	56.13	15	94,554	-
NEW MEXICO	286,417	47.85	-	286,783	47.91	5	21,251	-
NEW YORK	2,403,374	35.23	-	4,107,697	60.21	33	244,030	-
N. CAROLINA	1,631,163	56.03	14	1,257,692	43.2	-	0	-
N. DAKOTA	174,852	60.66	3	95,284	33.05	-	9,486	-
OHIO	2,351,209	49.97	21	2,186,190	46.46	-	117,857	-
OKLAHOMA	744,337	60.31	8	474,276	38.43	-	0	-
OREGON	713,577	46.52	-	720,342	46.96	7	77,357	-
PENNSYLVANIA	2,281,127	46.43	-	2,485,967	50.6	23	103,392	-
RHODE ISLAND	130,555	31.91	-	249,508	60.99	4	25,052	-
S. CAROLINA	785,937	56.83	8	565,561	40.91	-	20,200	-
S. DAKOTA	190,700	60.3	3	118,804	37.56	-	0	-
TENNESSEE	1,061,949	51.15	11	981,720	47.28	-	19,781	-
TEXAS	3,799,639	59.3	32	2,433,746	37.98	-	137,994	-
UTAH	515,096	66.83	5	203,053	26.34	-	35,850	-
VERMONT	119,775	40.7	-	149,022	50.63	3	20,374	-
VIRGINIA	1,437,490	52.47	13	1,217,290	44.44	-	59,398	-
WASHINGTON	1,108,864	44.56	-	1,247,652	50.13	11	103,002	-
WEST VIRGINIA	336,475	51.92	5	295,497	45.59	-	10,680	-
WISCONSIN	1,237,279	47.61	-	1,242,987	47.83	11	94,070	-
WYOMING	147,947	67.76	3	60,481	27.7	-	*4,625	-
	50,456,002	47.87%	271	50,999,897	48.38%	266	2,882,955	-

* Write-in Votes.

Source: State Elections Offices. http://www.fec.gov/pubrec/2000presgeresults.htm

As reports of these uncounted votes came in, Bush's lead over Gore narrowed and the networks again retracted their predictions, placing Florida in the undecided category. By midmorning the day after the election, Bush's lead had shrunk to about 500 votes statewide. Under Florida law a margin that small triggered an automatic recount. In addition to the mandated recount, Gore asked for a hand recount in four heavily Democratic counties.

By the day after the election, out-of-state lawyers from both parties intent on using the courts to win the election or at least prevent the other party from stealing it deluged Florida. Each side filed lawsuits—the Gore camp demanding recounts and the Bush team seeking to stop the recounts. For thirty-five days, the nation watched as recounts proceeded, then were stopped by court orders only to start up again.

As the litigation proceeded, Americans were introduced to a new term: chad. A "chad" is the little piece of cardboard that is supposed to be removed from a ballot as a voter pushes a stylus through the hole next to a candidate's name. Unfortunately, for a variety of reasons, a voter may not successfully punch out a chad entirely. If this is the case, the card reader does not record a vote. As Americans learned, failure to dislodge the chad can result in a dimpled chad, a pregnant chad, or a hanging chad. The law in Florida, as in most states, required that those counting the votes make every effort to interpret the voters' intentions, but the vote counters were prohibited from assuming the voters' choice. The law gave little guidance as to how to count ballots with dimpled, pregnant, and dangling chads. Thus the controversial recounts were carried on amid a great deal of uncertainty as to how the ballots should be treated.

The legal wrangling took place in several courts, until finally on December 12 the U.S. Supreme Court ruled that the multiple procedures for recounting votes in Florida was a violation of the Fourteenth Amendment and ordered an end to the process, just six days before the Electoral College was scheduled to meet.

With the Supreme Court decision, Gore conceded the election to Bush who won Florida by 537 votes and thus the presidency. Gore, for his part, won a plurality of the national vote (48.38 percent), but the 537-vote loss in Florida denied him a majority in the Electoral College. Ralph Nader and the Green Party placed third with 2.73 percent of the national votes, but potentially—and more importantly—Nader attracted over 97,000 votes in Florida. Democrats argued that those votes would have gone to Gore were Nader not on the ballot. Buchanan and the Reform Party had fewer than half a million votes nationwide, but to the Democrats' chagrin, he pulled 17,000 votes in Florida mostly from solidly Democratic precincts that used the confusing butterfly ballot.

Bush: How He Could Have Lost the 2000 Election

Al Gore began the 2000 election year well behind Bush in the polls, trailing 10–15 points in the spring. Gore was slowly building support through much of the spring and summer. By the time of the conventions, most surveys indicated that he had narrowed the gap and had approximately 47-percent support. After the Democratic convention, when an expected boost in popularity gave Gore some momentum, he was already in the lead heading into the fall campaign. Journalists and pundits began to draw parallels with 1988, when Vice President George H. W. Bush defeated Michael Dukakis by a comfortable margin. Some similarities between these two races were obvious: the incumbent vice president was in the lead, the economy appeared strong, and there was no major or lingering international conflict to deal with. Yet something began to change this perfect picture in September. Opinion polls revealed a slow but steady decline in Gore's support that continued to only days before the election. Professional forecasters on television and reporters had engaged in a two-month long guessing game leading up to the election. Nothing was clear in terms of the expected outcome. The only shared opinion was that this could be a very close race. In fact, it was the closest presidential election in U.S. history.

Textbooks conveniently mention Florida as the state where all the electoral drama took place. However, Bush could have lost the 2000 election for a host of different reasons.

RALPH NADER DROPS OUT OF THE RACE

Imagine a headline appearing in newspapers and across computer screens in September 2000: "Ralph Nader Drops Out of the Race"! In that event, almost three million potential voters—all of the initial Nader backers—would have had to have made up their own minds about how to vote in November. Assuming all of these people were rational voters making reasonable decisions on Election Day, then anyone's calculation would have been that Al Gore—without Nader on the ballot—would have easily achieved a sizable victory in the national polls. Newspapers and blog commentators, and then the leading experts in political science journals, all were certain about this outcome.[1] Most analyses were focusing on Florida and using simple statistics based on down-to-earth assumptions. Nader received approximately 97,000 votes in Florida. Exit polls showed that about 47 percent of the people who voted for Nader said that, if Nader had not been a candidate, they could have voted for Gore, and only 21 percent of the people who voted for Nader said they would have cast their ballots for Bush. In other words, if Nader had not run and all the people who voted for him had voted for one of the major candidates, Gore would have received some 24,000 extra votes to top Bush. Using similar assumptions and exit polls, critics also maintained that had Nader not run, Gore could have won New Hampshire as well. His victory in that state would have provided enough electoral votes for him to win presidency.

All these arguments seem reasonable assuming that Nader supporters voted after he left the race. According to exit polls, about one third of those who voted for Nader said they would have stayed home if Nader was not on the ballot. While there were other candidates in different states, including Florida, who took votes away from Gore, his national victory in the absence of Nader would have been very probable. Nader took the election away from Gore.

BUSH LOSES IN NEW HAMPSHIRE

If George Bush lost in New Hampshire and the voting results in other states had not been influenced by some extraordinary events, Gore would have been elected president. Even though New Hampshire had become a solid Republican stronghold since that late 1990s, Bush won in New Hampshire by a very slim margin of 7,211 votes. He did not even win a majority. His major opponents, Gore and Nader, received a combined 51 percent of the vote. Nader, as in Florida, came under criticism for his role as a spoiler in New Hampshire. Of approximately 22,000 people who voted for Nader, at least 8,000, according to estimations based on polls, would have voted for Gore if Nader has not been on the ballot. According to an analysis of the election results by the Republican campaign advisers, Bush won New Hampshire by an average margin of 24 votes per precinct. Statistically this means that it took only two dozen people per precinct to decide the election. Imagine, if a few more people had voted for Gore in each precinct, President Bush would have lost nationally.[2]

GORE WINS TENNESSEE

The third bitter pill to swallow for the Gore campaign, in addition to Nader and New Hampshire, was the fact that Gore failed to win the popular vote in his home state, Tennessee, which both he and his father had represented in the Senate for a total of twenty-six years. He lost by about 80,000 votes, which at first appears to be a large margin, but in fact represents roughly 0.4 percent of the almost two million votes cast. Had he won Tennessee, the Florida results would not have mattered.

Focusing on Florida, the media in 2000 did not portray the results in Tennessee as a big surprise. Yet Gore's disappointing performance was a historic anomaly. Why? Gore was the first major-party presidential candidate in the last quarter of a century to have lost his home state. The last time was in 1972 when George McGovern lost in his native state South Dakota. Other presidential candidates were more successful in this regard. Jimmy Carter in 1980, while defeated nationally, still managed to win his state of Georgia by an impressive 236,000. Walter Mondale won Minnesota by 4,000 votes despite losing to Reagan overall in 1984. Michael Dukakis won in Massachusetts in 1988 by more than 200,000 thousand votes. Similarly, George Bush won Texas in 1992, and Bob Dole won big in Kansas in 1996.

Gore might have said, "Thank you, Tennessee!" if he had returned to his home state after a successful election. Instead, his team was left trying to determine what went wrong.

Monica Lewinsky Wasn't There

Al Gore could have been justified to believe that only one person had cost him the presidency. This person was the White House intern, Monica Lewinsky. The Lewinsky scandal captured the attention of the nation and tarnished the reputation of Bill Clinton and many people associated with him.

In March 1999, forty percent of American households watching television on a Wednesday night tuned in to ABC to see Lewinsky interviewed by Barbara Walters. The host asked her many questions and broached many personal topics, including the excitement of phone sex with the president of the United States. With an audience of 48,530,000 viewers over the two hours of the telecast, this interview became the most-watched news program ever broadcast by a single network in television history.

When the scandal broke out a year earlier, tales about Clinton's personal life overshadowed all other news. For example, between Labor Day and Election Day in 1998, the number of stories about the election appearing on network evening news was 72. During the same period, the number of stories about Monica Lewinsky was 426. In December 1998, major media sources published 182 articles about taxes and 59 about terrorism. The Lewinsky scandal was covered in 1,613 stories.[3]

Controversial stories elevated in significance by the media could bring down almost any political career. One of the most prominent reminders is the case of former U.S. Senator Gary Hart, a major contender for the 1988 Democratic presidential nomination. While rebuffing journalists' questions about a suspected extramarital affair, he challenged the press to "catch" him. The challenge was accepted. As a result, the senator's affair was exposed on the front pages of leading newspapers and on primetime television news. This unexpected publicity forced Hart to drop out of the presidential race. Accusations of sexual harassment created enormous media hype around Clarence Thomas's Supreme Court nomination in 1991. In 2001, the widely debated facts in the media about inappropriate behavior with an intern ended the political career of the powerful California Representative Gary Condit. And for Gore in the late 1990s, the Lewinsky scandal adversely affected the image of the president and forced Gore to distance himself from Clinton during the 2000 campaign.

As Vice President Nixon had done forty years earlier in 1960, Al Gore struggled to carve out his own distinct political profile. The difference was that Nixon failed to take advantage of the goodwill left behind by his predecessor, President Eisenhower. Gore, however, could not easily escape the infamy associated with his boss in the White House. While most Americans approved of Bill Clinton as president, most voters viewed him unfavorably as a person in 2000. Critical feelings about Clinton personally cut Gore's support among those who approved of Clinton's job as president from 85 percent to 63 percent.

Gore lost the election partially because of Bill Clinton's personal mistakes. Trying not to be associated with Clinton's image, Gore appeared too uncharismatic, ineffective as a debater, and as a candidate who was constantly re-inventing himself. To many people he appeared a robot trapped in a human's body. As an anonymous Web commentator put it not long ago, "The Al Gore who ran for president in 2000 was not the rock star Al Gore of today."

GORE WINS BY STRESSING THE ECONOMY

In August 2000, political scientists used several forecasting models to estimate Gore's probability of winning the popular vote in November. Overall, the probability was 90 percent.[4] Moreover, a group of election forecasters who gathered at the 2000 Annual Meeting of the American Political Science Association offered statistical predictions that Gore would win a plurality of the two-party popular vote that ranged from an impressive 52.8 percent to a spectacular 60.3 percent.[5] Obviously, these predictions were wrong.

Does this mean that political science is incapable of accurate predictions? In self-defense, forecasters maintained that the problem was not with the forecasting models but, most likely, with Al Gore as a candidate. In short, as one review put it bluntly, Gore was "a flawed candidate who squandered a prime opportunity to capture the White House."[6] In fact, many computational studies of presidential elections suggest that Gore, in theory, should have won in 2000. Research shows that voters leave the candidate from the incumbent party in the White House if at least two conditions are met: the economy is good throughout the election year and the presidential party is not feuding from within. In 2000, Gore had these two favorable conditions.

When the economy is strong, the incumbent party candidate emphasizes this fact in the campaign relentlessly. Reagan did in 1984, and Clinton did the same in 1996. In the spring of 2000, the economy was in good shape, and most economic indicators were stronger than four years earlier. All of the predictive election models expected Gore to make the economy the centerpiece of his message. Gore's campaign did not. Gore did not stress the strong economy. Moreover, he downplayed the nation's economic prosperity. Rather than running a campaign emphasizing his—or President Clinton's—past success, Gore was preoccupied with arguments about the future. He later engaged in a divisive campaign moving to the left from the ideological center. In fact, Gore said in his nomination acceptance speech at the Democratic convention: "This election is not an award for past performance. I'm not asking you to vote for me on the basis of the economy we have." Gore, of course, discussed the status of the economy, but he certainly emphasized it less often than he discussed the future, including his plans to guarantee prescription drug benefits, enact tax cuts, and create various "lock boxes" to save Social Security. In these discussions, Gore was almost on equal footing with Bush.[7] If he had emphasized to voters the good economic times that they had with the previous president, this would have added a few percentage points to his total in November.

IF ECONOMIC CONDITIONS WERE SLIGHTLY BETTER

A few leading political scientists and economists still maintain that there was nothing fundamentally wrong with Gore's political campaign. In their view, he did as well as he could under the circumstances. One important development, however, could have influenced the opinions of the voters, especially the uncommitted and independent. What was it?

Remember, the most important basis for optimism about a possible Gore win was the perception that the nation was in the midst of an unmatched period of economic prosperity. Yet, in reality, the most significant economic indicators were never as favorable for the Democrats as observers believed in the months leading up to the 2000 election. News of the anemic performance of the stock market and rising gasoline prices dominated newspapers and television in the early fall. As a result, voters received much more negative news about the economy than would normally be expected given the broader economic picture. Again, this temporary effect of somewhat alarming economic news was exacerbated by Gore's aversion to running on the economic record of the Clinton administration.

To summarize, the long economic boom that arrived too late to have George H. W. Bush reelected in 1992 seems to have ended by 2000, which was not a good economic indicator for candidates running on the incumbent platform.[8] Had economic conditions been as favorable in 2000 as they were in 1999, Gore would have done about one-half to one percentage point better, almost certainly enough to win.

THE BALLOT IS NOT OF THE "BUTTERFLY" TYPE

The words "Berlin Wall," "Watergate," and "D-Day" have been in our vocabulary for some time. They have become common metaphors for ideological hostility, fraud, and bravery, respectively. If the term "butterfly ballot" survives the test of time, it should become the ultimate symbol for confusion. One of the most contentious aspects of the 2000 election is the design of the butterfly ballot used by the voters in Palm Beach County, Florida. Its design was so confusing that it affected the outcome of the presidential race. Some people who intended to vote for

Gore could not figure out how to mark their voting decisions correctly. Indeed, there were so many boxes and arrows on the ballot with directions on how to proceed that, as a result, if a voter did not pay careful attention he or she could have easily made an error. Because of the ballot's design, some voters accidentally voted not for Gore but for Patrick Buchanan simply because his name appeared close to Gore's. This mistake repeated hundreds of times might have been pivotal in determining the election outcome. These all are assumptions. Yet is there any serious evidence to support these claims?

Overall, about 2,000 Gore supporters may have mistakenly voted for Buchanan. Several experimental and statistical studies showed that because of the ballot's design, people who voted for Bush did not make this mistake. In general, Buchanan received almost 20 percent of his total statewide support in Palm Beach, which contains only about 7 percent of the voters in Florida.[9] Furthermore, the number of multiple-punched ballots in Palm Beach County (called *overvotes* and deemed invalid) was over 19,000. This number is unusually high compared to the returns from other Florida counties. Overall, there were about 50,000 discarded overvotes in Florida.[10] One of the explanations of such an irregularity was that many people punched their ballots incorrectly (they were confused by the ballot design). After they realized their mistake, they tried to punch a new hole. This voided the ballot. With the presidential election results in Florida depending on a difference of less than 1,000 votes, the butterfly ballot might have proved the difference in the national election.

No Exit Polls

Exit polls are supposed to be random surveys that show how an election is going and which candidates are currently ahead or trailing. In theory, exit polls, like scoreboards, show the dynamic of the election process. They are supposed to reflect, not to influence, anyone's behavior. Does the reporting of exit polls on Election Day influence the behavior of people who have not voted yet? Common sense suggests that there should be an effect. Specifically, in the 2000 election in Florida, major news organizations declared victory for Gore based on exit polls in Miami-Dade and other big counties. However, polls in western Florida, because this portion of the state is on Central Standard Time, were still open. Because of this early reporting, a sufficient number of Bush's supporters had probably heard the news about Gore's victory and did not go to the polls.[11]

However, behavioral research also shows that this argument has serious flaws. Most people do not choose only one strategy when they hear the projected results of elections. It is very possible that many voters who had planned to vote in western Florida had chosen not to vote because their candidate—Al Gore—had already won. After all, he was declared a winner by major television networks! Political psychologists show that part of our motivation to vote is based on the belief that our vote will be meaningful, that it will not be "wasted." Therefore, if the election was presumed to be over, many people would have chosen not to vote. The paradox of such assumptions is that if the networks announced that Bush had won Florida, scores of his supporters could have returned home without casting their ballots and this could have, in theory, brought more votes for Gore.

The debates about the early reporting in the Florida election caused significant changes to be made in electoral coverage. In congressional hearings in 2001, news executives from ABC, CBS, CNN, NBC, and the Associated Press outlined several changes for future election coverage. For example, the networks pledged not to declare the winner of any state's election until after all the polls have closed there. CNN said it would not project a winner when the margin of victory was less than one percent. ABC said it would insulate its own election analysts from other networks.

BUSH APPEARED MORE CONSERVATIVE

If during the campaign Gore had not moved to the left on various issues, and if Bush had not drifted toward the middle of the ideological spectrum, Gore might have become president. Bush's political profile did not appear as conservative in 2000 as some perceived it during his presidency. Analytical studies based on his campaign speeches and debate transcripts show that Bush, who emphasized tax cuts and education reform, was rated as somewhat closer to the center of American politics than Gore was. The Democratic candidate in 2000 began to move to the left emphasizing social inequality while criticizing corporations and big businesses. On Election Day, studies of exit polls also suggest that the public placed Gore further from the political center compared to Bush who was seen as closer to the middle.[12]

Studies of presidential elections of the past fifty years demonstrate that (contrary to some people's belief that to win, a candidate must be as ideological and partisan as possible) if a candidate appears more extreme, relative to his opponent, he will lose votes in November. In short, according to the studies, the closer to the center a candidate is, the more votes he will receive. Various statistical studies, for example, show that Barry Goldwater in 1964, George McGovern in 1972, and Ronald Reagan in 1980 would have gathered almost three additional percentage points of the popular vote if they had moved, in the eyes of the voters, to the center. Actually, these candidates did not have to do that. Reagan's margin of victory over Carter was 8.5 million. As for Goldwater and McGovern, candidates who lost their elections by 16 and 18 million votes respectively, the additional votes they would have received by moving to the center would not have helped. It could have been a different story in 2000 though. Had Gore appeared as moderate as Bush, as statistical models based on opinion polls show, he would have done more than half a percentage point better and almost certainly would have won, assuming all other variables remained the same.[13]

THERE IS NO INCUMBENT FATIGUE

Empirical studies of electoral behavior demonstrate that the number of consecutive terms the incumbent party has held the White House is, as a rule, a negative factor posing serious difficulty to the nominee from the incumbent party. The so-called incumbency model of electoral behavior suggests that after two or three consecutive terms in office, the candidate from the ruling party tends to witness his chances for reelection diminish significantly. In other words, in most recent history, parties seem to lose after eight years in office, only to return to power after two terms in opposition. Eisenhower, after eight years in the office, could not pass the baton to Nixon in 1960. Democrats, after two terms in the White House, lost the White House in 1968 to Nixon. Republicans, also after their two terms, surrendered power to Jimmy Carter in 1976. Republicans won again in 1988 after Reagan's two-term tenure expired, but lost to Clinton in 1992. In 2000, based on the incumbency model, the chances of a Republican victory were high. Bartels and Zaller call this phenomenon "incumbent-party fatigue"; it is also referred to as the "third-term penalty" by Abramowitz.[14] Thinking in counterfactual terms, had the Democrats been in office for only one term rather than two, Gore would have done about half a percentage point better in November, almost certainly enough to win.

Why does the incumbent-party fatigue happen? Critics say that the longer an incumbent party is in power, the more likely it is that strong leaders within the party will give way to less inspiring successors. In addition, the incumbent leaders have to deal with the heavy weight of political scandals, lingering problems, and other difficulties easily associated with the incumbency. This is exactly what happened to Nixon in 1960, Humphrey in 1968, Ford in 1976, and Bush in 1992. In addition, historically, open-seat presidential elections have been much more competitive. The chances of a near dead-heat election increase nearly five times in an open-seat race, and the chances of a landslide are less than half of what they are when an incumbent runs. It appears easier to convince voters that it is "time for a change" if the incumbent party has held the White House for at least two consecutive terms.

If Bush Were Not Elected

What if Al Gore were president? This question has become one of the most frequent subjects of discussions related to the contemporary presidency. Altogether, there are some 170 posted articles, detailed comments, and analytical opinions focused specifically on counterfactual thinking related to Gore as would-be president. Posted between 2001 and 2008, the vast majority of the materials, 105, are critical of George Bush and his presidency. Most of these articles contain emotional assessments of how different things could be if Al Gore were in the Oval Office. Conversely, some thirty publications are either mildly critical of Gore or unenthusiastic about what his possible performance might have looked like. The most common assumption in these articles is that Gore as president would have made even more mistakes than Bush has. In only five publications, Gore's unfulfilled presidency was assessed as disastrous. The remaining thirty or so publications see little difference between Gore and Bush as presidents.

Gore himself has suggested before a national audience what kind of a president he would have been if he had won the 2000 election. In May 2006, he did an opening skit on NBC's *Saturday Night Live*. The former vice president jokingly summarized what his major accomplishments would have been if he occupied the Oval Office. He said that he would have stopped global warming, and the American people would be paying significantly less for gasoline. He also said that he would have fixed Social Security, welfare, and would have established universal health care. He would have produced a federal budget surplus. In international affairs, world public opinion would have been overwhelmingly supportive of the United States. Afghanistan would be the most popular spring break destination, and Iran would have built a "Six Flags" theme park, the best in the world. He would have averted all natural disasters and would have solved the immigration problem. Film director Michael Moore would have been nominated for and won the vacant seat on the Supreme Court. George Clooney would have become chief justice of the United States. Finally, Gore said that he would have graciously recommended George Bush as commissioner of Major League Baseball. In other words, Gore, as he has stated, would have done much better in all areas of life, politics, and international relations.

DOMESTIC POLICIES

On the domestic front, Gore could have retained several top politicians and professionals from the Clinton circle. Larry Summers probably would not have moved to Harvard, but stayed in a top economic position. Robert Rubin would have returned to a cabinet post. New people, successful investors and CEOs such as Steven Rattner and Jim Johnson, would have been brought in as well.[15] There would not have been substantial tax cuts except for some temporary programs. Gore would have found a way to work with the Republican Congress. Since he would have been an interventionist president abroad, he would have received support for his domestic agenda. According to the popular two-level theory of foreign policy, state leaders frequently make political bargains with their domestic opposition: presidents and prime ministers receive the opposition's support for the government's current foreign policy in exchange for the leader's acceptance of the opposition's policies at home. These bargains could go the other way around. Thus, satisfying a more "hawkish" Republican Congress in terms of U.S. foreign policy, Gore would have received support for his domestic programs. Most probably, Gore would have focused on an economic stimulus packages to fuel the slowing economy of the early 2000s, and he would have created several federal programs to stimulate the economy.[16] He would also have extended unemployment benefits, pushed for minimum pay increases, and would have tried to strengthen labor unions to guarantee their support in the 2004 election. Most importantly, assuming that the circumstances had not changed, Gore would have nominated two justices to the Supreme Court, which might have led to a considerable change in the most significant judicial decisions in contemporary American history.

GORE AS A MODERATE-TO-HAWKISH PRESIDENT

Gore's foreign policy would have continued the policy established at the end of the Cold War and reinforced in the Clinton years. Top Democrats by 2000 had accepted that most elements of their foreign-policy initiatives started in the 1990s. They generally agreed on limited state building, a consistent but careful cooperation with the United Nations, and multilateral foreign policy, that is, the policy of multilateral action with allies. Considering similar circumstances, Bush and Gore were not much different in terms of the leading principles of foreign policy. Of course, Gore would not have used the services of Colin Powell, Dick Cheney, or Donald Rumsfeld. Dick Holbrooke, then the U.S. ambassador to the United Nations, might have become secretary of state. Sam Nunn, former Georgia senator, was mentioned as a possible secretary of defense. Leon Fuerth would have continued as Gore's national security adviser. These and other possible members of a Gore administration, including Senator George Mitchell and Warren Christopher, were experienced and effective foreign-policy experts. They might well have arrived at the same conclusions as the Bush foreign-policy team did. The main difference would have been the ideological framing of their actions. Gore would have refrained from assigning the U.S. foreign policy a "missionary" role. The term "neo-cons" would have been unknown to most Americans. Yet democracy promotion and nation building would be at the center of Gore's agenda, backed by pragmatic arguments.

Gore would have remained active on the foreign-policy front for one important political reason. If we assume that the U.S. Congress remained under Republican control, Gore as president would have been under constant pressure to conduct an active foreign policy, as all U.S. presidents did since Woodrow Wilson. America would have been actively engaged in various international crises in many parts of the world. Paradoxically, he would have faced resistance from the Republicans. Many historical examples suggest that the opposition party in Congress is typically suspicious of military engagements abroad that are unilaterally initiated by the president. In 1999, for instance, Republicans in the House of Representatives were very hesitant to support the NATO bombing campaign in Kosovo (initiated and supported by President Clinton). The main argument was that the bombing had not been sanctioned by the United Nations. Therefore, in the case of Gore, every mistake or unfortunate development taking place overseas would have been attributed by the Republican majority in Congress to the inherently "weak" Clinton-Gore policies. This could have been a tough time for President Gore. He would have had to fight on two fronts: one against the Republicans and the other against fellow Democrats accusing him of being a "Tennessee cowboy" and a Republican "puppet."

SEPTEMBER 11 AND AFGHANISTAN

All things being equal, there is a commonly held opinion by the vast majority of commentators that the events of 9/11 were unavoidable regardless of the occupant in the White House. (Conspiracy theories about the origins of September 11 and the Bush administration's involvement in the terrorist acts are not plausible enough to consider them seriously here.) No matter who the president was, the planning of the terrorist operation against America was underway. Osama bin Laden had announced Al Qaeda's major political objectives back in the late 1990s, and there was nothing in Gore's character or his policy record to indicate that he would have tried to accommodate and appease any radical group. Bin Laden, for example, demanded that Washington stop supporting Israel. He also demanded that the U.S. military get out of Saudi Arabia and other Arab countries. Finally, his major demand was that America stop supporting authoritarian leaders in the Arab world, specifically the royal dynasties in Saudi Arabia, Jordan, and the Gulf States.[17] In reality, that support had been part of U.S. foreign policy for more than several decades. Based on U.S. policies in the Middle East alone, the most logical conclusion is that Bin Laden or his followers would have carried on with their deadly missions. Suggestions that Gore and his advisers might have better understood the seriousness of the threat from Islamic fundamentalism so that they would have had better opportunities to prevent the terrorist acts are largely wishful thinking.

As president, Gore might have ordered military operations in Afghanistan in the fall and winter of 2001. If he had not done this immediately following 9/11, he would have come under tremendous pressure from the Republican opposition and some interventionists from his own party, including senators from New York, Connecticut, and New Jersey, the three states with populations that suffered directly from the attacks. Most probably, regardless of the timing of Gore's response, the congressional opposition and other Republican leaders would have criticized the Gore administration for the delays and indecisiveness. However, criticism would not have led to serious partisan attacks in times of "rallying around the flag" late in 2001 and in 2002. As a result, suggestions that the Republican Congress would have impeached Gore for poor performance after September 11 are unfounded.

However, it is quite probable that Gore would have built up a bigger and more efficient international coalition to conduct operations in Afghanistan. Specifically, he would have reached an agreement with Moscow about a more significant participation of the Russian military in the conflict in exchange for broad security guarantees and a non-critical U.S. position related to the Russia's aggressive policies in the breakaway republic of Chechnya.

WAR IN IRAQ

It was a long-term goal of two presidential administrations in the 1990s to remove Saddam Hussein from power in Iraq or significantly diminish his influence. Al Gore would have to have pursued the similar policy and would have applied pressure against Iraq however he could. Nevertheless, it is not an impossible scenario that Hussein would have attempted to approach the United States and offer some form of a deal, similar to what he had offered to the allied countries during his invasion of Kuwait in 1990. Saddam would have offered to play an increasingly key role in the Middle East as an intimidating force against Iran's fundamentalist regime. In exchange for this role, however, the Iraqi dictator would have received relatively more freedom to operate within his country and dominate the entire region. Probably, some economic sanctions against Iraq would have been lifted.

These possibilities should not be a surprise because they relate to one of the most important foreign-policy principles of any powerful country, including the United States. Support of "friendly" dictators has been a prevalent policy of the twentieth century. Hussein could not have brokered any deal with George W. Bush for a number of reasons, the most important of which were personal and political. Although Gore was part of the Clinton team that continued the policies of Bush senior, Gore did not have any personal animosity against Saddam or deeply seated ideological conviction to get rid of the Iraqi ruler. A deal with Iraq would have been interpreted by Vice President Lieberman as an important step to provide security relief for Israel. To some extent, Russia, very much interested in maintaining its own presence in the Middle East, could have played a larger, friendlier role in this region helping the United States to strike a seemingly fair deal with Baghdad. That would have served to bolster the view of the United States in world public opinion. Similar bargains worked in the past for some time; therefore, there was a possibility that a new deal would have lasted at least temporarily. As a result, there would have been no war in Iraq.

Conclusion

Trying to move through the political center and hoping for his reelection in 2004, Gore would have tried to retain the support of the independents and moderate Republicans. This centrist position would have caused resentment from many liberal Democrats, especially those groups that believed that they had put Gore in the White House in 2000. Take environmental policies, for example. There is more than ample evidence to assume that Gore would not have developed an activist position on the issue of global climate change. In 1997, the Senate unanimously passed the Byrd-Hegel resolution against the ratification of the Kyoto protocol that would have reduced America's carbon emissions. President Clinton did not submit the protocol to the Senate for ratification. Moreover, Gore also indicated that the protocol should have dealt with broader issues and not forced the economically advanced countries to cut emissions unilaterally, while other nations would have increased them. Gore also would have had difficulties domestically to become a "green" president pursuing restrictive environmental policies without alienating substantial political support in key industrial states. Moreover, many critics suggest that Gore would have been preoccupied with so many smaller but urgent problems that he would have moved environmental issues to the back burner for some time.[18]

If the United States were involved in a war in Afghanistan and several smaller conflicts elsewhere, Gore would have also faced opposition within his own party.[19] Two developments were possible here. On the one hand, Gore's policies would have caused divisions and a radicalization of a portion of his political base. Serious debates about the future of the Democratic Party and American liberalism in general would have continued through 2004. If a serious candidate emerged from the left wing of the party, the Democrats would have lost the White House. As you remember, if an incumbent party is split across ideological lines during the election year, this is a serious factor signaling a potential loss of the White House. On the other hand, and this is a more plausible scenario, under Gore the Democrats would have created a moderate and centrist platform that would have incorporated several conservative economic principles (thus "stealing" them from the Republican Party). Among such principles would have been a strong foreign policy, robust military policies, and a moderate social agenda at home. By 2004, Gore would have built up a foundation for a new and long-term political realignment within the United States. As with Nixon in 1968, Gore would have attracted a significant number of votes in the South by staying in the middle and offering commonsense policies at home and abroad. Among the permanent swing states in the South would have been Virginia, North Carolina, and Florida—quite enough to guarantee Gore's reelection in 2004.

Conclusion

A lesson of history is that we cannot reverse it. Whatever happened is already part of our lives. Yet when we re-examine the events of the past or when we imagine something that hasn't happen, we can draw new lessons from both. Lost opportunities and unrealized possibilities, polices never pursued, speeches never delivered, and one hundred voters who never appeared at the polls—all those "would be" scenarios teach us to appreciate the splendor and power of a single moment. Every day of our lives is loaded with unpredictability and certainty—the two transcendental elements of tomorrow.

Studying the great events of the past, we did not want to bring retrospective arrogance to the process. We simply wanted to show that close elections were not only exercises in preference ordering but responses to a specific electoral environment and concrete circumstances surrounding the country at a certain point in time.

Staying the Course

It seems that, in many respects, those extremely close elections of the past had a negligible impact on the course of history. Very often, the winner of the White House managed to swing from the extremes of electoral rhetoric to the middle ground of actual policies. In 1801, in his inaugural address, President Jefferson prominently said, "We are all Republicans, we are all Federalists." As if following up on this, Jefferson regularly acted like a Federalist even as he espoused Republican principles. As Hamilton said, President Jefferson was not the radical that Federalists had assumed him to be.

It is clear today how little the candidates Hayes and Tilden actually disagreed on the major issues facing the country in 1876. In fact, both candidates were politically moderate governors from northern states who were fiscal conservatives, interested in government reform, and making plans to end Reconstruction.

In 1916, both candidates, Wilson and Hughes, were faithful social progressives who supported an active role for government in many areas of life, including social welfare, employment, and education. They both emphasized the importance of moral values, social justice, science, and education. Both wanted to see America strong in international affairs and neither one of the two could have prevented the passage of the Eighteenth Amendment to the Constitution banning the manufacture, transport, and sale of intoxicating liquors. It seems that America would have gone through the period of self-imposed prohibition no matter who the president was.

In 1960, if Nixon were president, he would have—like Kennedy—conducted a robust, interventionist foreign policy based on the traditional values of a strong military, support of friendly nations, and containment of adversaries, the Soviet Union in particular. Nixon could not have prevented the Vietnam War, and he, like Kennedy, would have resisted the escalating pressures from the Soviet Union and China.

If Humphrey were elected in 1968, he would have probably espoused domestic policies similar to Nixon's. The difference between him and Nixon would have been that Humphrey would have tried certain social policies but failed to implement them due to the fierce partisan congressional opposition. Nixon simply did not attempt these policies. Other initiatives, such as a universal health care plan, which Nixon tried to advance at one time, would have also faced fierce congressional opposition and would have ultimately failed.

After 2000, if Al Gore were elected president, the Democrats would have created a moderate and clearly centrist platform that would have incorporated several conservative economic principles (thus disarming the Republican Party). Among such principles would have been a strong foreign policy, a robust military, free trade in the global arena, and a fiscally responsible social agenda at home.

There are many possibilities that these closest elections could have turned history in a distinctively new way.

History Turned

If Adams had been elected president, political opposition to the Louisiana Purchase in Congress would have been so fierce that it would have discouraged Adams from even trying it out of fear of being accused of squandering the national budget. Imagine the United States without its western states today and North America, as a continent, comprised of five or six independent countries.

In 1876, if Tilden were elected president, he, as the winner of the popular vote, would not have been called an illegitimate president—a serious charge that dogged president Hayes for years. Second, unlike Hayes, Tilden never promised to be a one-term president. Most likely, he would have sought a second term and won it. Under this quite probable scenario, James Garfield would have remained a congressman, would never have run for the presidency, been elected, and been attacked by an assassin.

America under President Hughes, if he were elected in 1916, would have been an active member of the League of Nations, restraining small and belligerent states, establishing new zones of influence, and planting the seeds of interventionism around the world. Hughes would have also developed somewhat friendly relations with Imperial Japan, and this would have probably postponed for twenty-five years a military confrontation with Tokyo, thus altering the dynamics of World War II. Imagine there were no Pearl Harbor, the battle for Iwo Jima had never taken place, there were no D-Day, and no mushroom clouds over Hiroshima and Nagasaki.

Imagine, in 1961, newly elected President Richard Nixon would not have allowed the Bay of Pigs operation against Cuba to get out of hand. He also would have negotiated the situation around Berlin by accepting its international status, thus avoiding a major confrontation with the Soviets. He would have probably contained the Castro regime by making secret deals with the communists.

Yet Nixon lost the election of 1960. When he was back to power in 1968, he brought on his shoulders a new conservative political wave, which would have been tempered if Humphrey had won the election. Without the Watergate scandal and a national backlash against Nixon, Reagan's rise to power in 1980 probably would have not taken place. Alternatively, as president, Humphrey, most probably, would have been able to consolidate the Democratic Party, which could have stayed in power for a considerable time afterwards. Humphrey would have also continued with ambitious space exploration plans inherited from Kennedy. He would have endorsed the establishment of a permanent base on the moon by the end of the 1970s and the launch of a manned expedition to Mars as early as the 1980s.

Likewise, if Gore prevailed in 2000, he would have built up a solid foundation for a new and long-term political realignment within the United States, which would have favored the Democratic Party for at least a decade. Like Richard Nixon in 1968, Gore would have attracted a significant number of votes in the South by staying in the political middle and offering commonsense policies at home and abroad.

No Violence

Close elections revealed another remarkable trend in American politics: none of the closest presidential elections in the United States resulted in violent protests or organized resistance and disobedience. Nor has a nationwide paralyzing crisis occurred. Only in 1800 was the country very close to such a crisis, and warnings against possible violence were disseminated on the highest level. The election of 1800 truly was a crucial moment in American history. It is hard to underestimate how close the Constitution came to failing. Yet the Constitution survived and open hostilities never materialized.

Globally, in similar situations when national presidential elections result in uncertainty, people frequently turn to violent actions.

Just a few examples from the most recent history show how easily political parties call for disobedience and the street erupts if people perceive the outcome of their country's national elections unfair. In 2004, Ukraine was paralyzed in the wake of its presidential election. In 2006, Mexico was on the brink of a significant national crisis following its presidential election. Kenya plunged into rampant violence in 2007. Armenia declared a state of emergency in 2008 following mass riots and civilian casualties.

Electoral "Fundamentals"

Results of close elections have also confirmed several fact-based "fundamentals" that are supposed to play a predictable role in shaping presidential election outcomes.[1] What are these fundamentals?

The incumbency factor. From 1951, when the Twenty-second Amendment to the U.S. Constitution went into effect, the party that has spent two terms in the White House is set to lose the next presidential election. The only exception to this was Michael Dukakis's defeat in 1988, when he lost to Bush senior who had spent eight years as vice president. However, Nixon, who also spent two terms as vice president in the Eisenhower administration, had lost in 1960. Vice President Hubert Humphrey could not extend the Democratic Party's control of the White House in 1968. Similarly, in three other cases, the candidates representing two-term party incumbents lost: Ford in 1976, Bush senior in 1992, and Gore in 2000 were the "victims" of the incumbency factor.

The economy factor. A poorly performing economy and, most importantly, a negative perception of the economy by the American public, indicated in opinion polls, reduces the chance for reelection of the party occupying the White House. This holds true regardless of whether the president runs for reelection or not. In the post–World War II era, in terms of the country's economic troubles, the elections generally have not been close and the candidate representing the White House has lost. Like Reagan in 1976, Clinton used the perception of a poor economy to defeat Bush in 1992. Gore in 2000 seemingly lost an opportunity to emphasize the strength of the economy under Clinton's watch. Again, public reflections of the economy's strengths and weaknesses matter.

National polls after Labor Day. The results of national surveys after Labor Day are likely to suggest which candidate will be elected two months later. In the six elections prior to 2000 in which the candidate representing the party in the White House had the support of 52 percent or more of Gallup Poll respondents around Labor Day, that candidate went on to win in all six cases. In other cases, uncertainty by the Labor Day means uncertainty in the polls.

Presence of a third candidate. Serious third-party candidates commonly grab the votes from both parties, yet they receive the most from the candidates whose ideological views are closest to theirs. In the past fifty years, John Anderson in 1980 was the only third-party candidate who did not substantially affect the results of the election. Other prominent third-party candidates, however, did play an important role including George Wallace in 1968, Ross Perot in 1992, and Ralph Nader in 2000.

A major war or international confrontation. An ongoing war is a powerful and highly circumstantial factor that could sway the election either way. In 1916, America's non-involvement in World War I helped Woodrow Wilson to get reelected. Franklin D. Roosevelt won in 1940 because he reflected the American public's unwillingness to go to war. He won in a landslide. In 1944, however, he won again, decisively, but this time as a war president. The wars in Korea in 1952 and Vietnam in 1968 were politically costly for the candidates representing the incumbent party in power: the Democratic candidates, Stevenson and Humphrey, respectively, lost in both cases. However, Nixon in 1972 won the election despite the ongoing war in Vietnam. Similarly, the unpopular war in Iraq, contrary to many predictions, was not a strong enough factor to defeat the incumbent President Bush in 2004.

Candidate's age. Historically, younger candidates running on the platform of "change" win against older candidates running on a more "preserve what is best" platform. Since 1960, Kennedy, Nixon, Carter, and Clinton all ran on the platform of change, and they all were younger than their opponents (Nixon, Humphrey, Ford, and Bush senior, respectively). Speaking allegorically, when change is the order of the day, it may be better to be a younger presidential candidate.

Candidate's occupation. In 1876, both presidential candidates were former governors (Ohio and New York). In 1916, again, two former governors (New York and New Jersey) competed for the White House. Since the 1960s, candidates who have been southern governors tended to win their match-ups against other non-governors. Carter, Clinton, and Bush junior were all southern governors who won their races five times (1976, 1992, 1996, 2000, and 2004) running against incumbent presidents (twice), senators (twice), and one vice president.

Public opinion about the incumbent. Low approval ratings of the incumbent president (even if he does not run) reduce the chances of his party winning the White House again. In other words, a successful term(s) by the incumbent president helps the candidate of the president's party and disadvantages the candidate of the opposition party.

Running from the center. Candidates leaning toward the center have a better chance to win compared to candidates moving "left" or "right" during the election campaign. In 1916, Wilson held the ideological "middle" and Hughes failed to distinguish himself. A few decades later, being on the opposite ends of the political spectrum, Goldwater in 1964 and, similarly, McGovern in 1972 lost because they both ran on intensely ideological platforms positioned far from the center. Kennedy in 1960 moved to the political "middle" and won, as did Nixon in 1968 running on the "order and stability" platform. The centrist motto of "compassionate conservatism" apparently helped George Bush in 2000.

A Few People Can Decide the Election

Historically, political parties in the United States have been less organized, disciplined, and cohesive than most of their counterparts in other countries. Therefore, issues that are important during the election year but are not necessarily part of a candidate's partisan platform may become a crucial factor in people's voting. In the last few decades, partisanship has become increasingly likely to be based not on long-term ideological attachments but rather on a person's approval or disapproval of specific policies. The parties' programs on issues—such as taxation, education, or immigration policies—may have a more significant impact on a voter's party identification than the voter's long-term partisan attachments. However, one of the most difficult tasks in predicting American elections is to determine who among voters remain "standpatters," those who will continue to support the same party during the next election, and how many become "switchers," those who will move next time to another party. In 1876, the presidency was decided purely along the partisan votes of the ad hoc Electoral Commission. In 1916, many Republicans voted for the Democrat Wilson alleging that their candidate Hughes was not "progressive" enough. In 1960, many young people, first-time voters from the Republican strongholds, chose Kennedy. In 1968, scores of Democrats worried about traditional values cast their ballots for Nixon. Reagan in 1980 won almost a quarter of the Jewish vote, a group that historically tends to vote Democratic. Likewise, Bush in 2000 won almost half of the Latino vote nationwide, exceeding all forecasts.[2]

Especially crucial in every election is now the vote of the young and those who vote for the first time. People who know more about life around them are more likely to vote than those who know less.[3] More knowledgeable people know more specific details about the country and the world around them, and about where and when to vote. Poorly informed citizens hold fewer, less stable, and less consistent opinions about candidates than those who are better informed. Research of the past two decades indicates that the overwhelming majority of the most knowledgeable ten percent Americans vote. In contrast, only a small portion of the least informed Americans cast their ballots.

It is quite probable that the most informed ten percent among us are those who actually elect the next president.

NOTES

INTRODUCTION

1. Leslie H. Gelb, *The Irony of Vietnam: The System Worked*, with Richard K. Betts (Washington, DC: Brookings Institution, 1979), 272–90.
2. James D. Barber, *The Presidential Character: Predicting Performance in the White House* (Englewood Cliffs, NJ: Prentice Hall, 1985), 7–11.
3. While turnout in national elections in most European democratic countries is higher than that in the United States, it also has declined. In the 1960s, an average of more than 85 percent of eligible voters in Western Europe—nearly 90 percent in both Germany and the Netherlands—cast their votes in national elections. But the rates have declined consistently. As of today, a sizable group of European countries (including Austria, Finland, Iceland, the Netherlands, Sweden, and Great Britain) recorded their lowest national election turnouts in fifty years; the rate has fallen below 80 percent for the first time since the end of World War II in 1945. Switzerland had the lowest turnout: less than four out of ten eligible voters there typically participated in the most recent national elections. Especially low numbers of voter participation are seen in European parliament elections: between 24 and 50 percent. Of course, there are countries that produce more favorable voting records. For example, in Belgium, where voting is compulsory, the turnout is high. Malta now records one of the highest and consistent turnouts of any democracy. See Eric Shiraev and Richard Sobel, *People and Their Opinions: Thinking Critically about Public Opinion* (New York: Pearson/Longman, 2006), 230–32.
4. Newsweek/Princeton conducted this survey on November 9–10, 2000, http://www.ropercenter.uconn.edu.
5. Edward Carr, *What is History?* (New York: St. Martin's Press, 1961), 3; Philip Tetlock, Richard Lebow, and Geoffrey Perker, eds., *Unmaking the West: "What If" Scenarios That Rewrite History* (Ann Arbor: University of Michigan Press, 2006), 3–6.
6. Fred Greensteen, "The Impact of Personality on the End of the Cold War," *Political Psychology* 19, no. 1 (1998): 1–16.

CHAPTER 1: 1800: THE ELECTION—A SECOND AMERICAN REVOLUTION?

1. John Ferling, *Adams vs. Jefferson: The Tumultuous Election of 1800* (New York: Oxford University Press, 2004), 94.
2. Included in this number is Massachusetts, which provided that the state legislature appoint two electors; the remaining electors were chosen by the state legislature from the top two vote-getters in district elections.
3. New Hampshire provided for selection in a statewide election, but if no candidate won a majority, the state legislature would appoint from the top two candidates.
4. Edward J. Larson, *A Magnificent Catastrophe* (New York: Free Press, 2007), 62–65.
5. Ibid., 60.
6. Ferling, *Adams vs. Jefferson*, 131.

CHAPTER 2: 1876: HAYES DEFEATS TILDEN—A COMMISSION DECIDES

1. Roy Morris, Jr., *Fraud of the Century: Rutherford B. Hayes, Samuel Tilden, and the Stolen Election of 1876* (New York: Simon & Schuster, 2003), 25.
2. Paul Leland Haworth, *The Hayes-Tilden Disputed Presidential Election of 1876* (Cleveland: Burrows Brothers Company, 1906), 31.
3. The Bland-Allison Act committed the United States to buy two to four million dollars worth of silver a month and to coin it at a ratio of 16:1 (16 ounces of silver to equal one ounce of gold).
4. *Historical Statistics of the United States, Colonial Times to 1970* (Washington, DC: U.S. Bureau of the Census, 2003).

CHAPTER 3: 1916: WILSON DEFEATS HUGHES—NO WAR, NOT YET

1. John Kendrick, *Productivity Trends in the United States* (Princeton: Princeton University Press, 1961).
2. Don D. Walker, "Woodrow Wilson and Walter Lippmann: A Narrative of Historical Imagery," *Western Political Quarterly* 12, no. 4 (December 1959): 939–47.
3. Margot Louria, "The Boldness of Charles Evan Hughes," *The National Interest*, June 22, 2003, 110–14; Margot Louria, *Triumph and Downfall: America's Pursuit of Peace and Prosperity, 1921–1933* (Westport, CT: Greenwood Press, 2001).
4. Merlo J. Pusey, *Charles Evans Hughes* (New York: Macmillan, 1951), 345–50.
5. Pendleton Herring, "Woodrow Wilson, Then and Now," *PS: Political Science & Politics* 7, no. 3 (Summer, 1974): 256–59; Alexander George and Juliette George, *Woodrow Wilson and Colonel House: A Personality Study* (New York: J. Day, 1956).
6. Walter Lippmann, *Men of Destiny* (New York: Macmillan, 1927), 130–37.

7. Kurt Wimer, "Woodrow Wilson's Plans to Enter the League of Nations through an Executive Agreement," *Western Political Quarterly* 11, no. 4 (December 1958): 800–12.

8. D. F. Fleming, "Woodrow Wilson and Collective Security Today," *Journal of Politics* 18, no. 4 (November 1956): 611–24.

9. James Henretta, "Charles Evans Hughes and the Strange Death of Liberal America," *Law and History Review* 24, no. 1 (2006): http://www.historycooperative.org/journals/lhr/24.1/henretta.html.

10. Pusey, *Charles Evans Hughes*, 384–87.

11. K. Narizny, "Both Guns and Butter, or Neither: Class Interests in the Political Economy of Rearmament," *American Political Science Review* 97, no. 2 (2003): 203–20.

12. Henry Turner, "Woodrow Wilson and Public Opinion," *The Public Opinion Quarterly* 21, no. 4 (Winter 1957–58): 505–20.

CHAPTER 4: 1960: KENNEDY DEFEATS NIXON—NO RECOUNTS

1. Philip Converse, "The Nature of Belief Systems in Mass Publics," in *Ideology and Discontent*, ed. D. E. Apter (London: Free Press, 1964), 206–61.

2. Theodore White, *The Making of the President, 1960* (New York: Atheneum, 1961).

3. Barber, *The Presidential Character*, 323–27.

4. Shiraev and Sobel, *People and Their Opinions*, 200–203.

5. Lawrence R. Jacobs and Robert Y. Shapiro, "Issues, Candidate Image, and Priming: The Use of Private Polls in Kennedy's 1960 Presidential Campaign," *American Political Science Review* 88, no. 3 (September 1994): 527–40.

6. Richard Reeves, *President Kennedy: Profiles of Power* (New York: Simon & Schuster, 1994), 14.

7. Anna K. Nelson, "President Kennedy's National Security Policy: A Reconsideration," *Reviews in American History* 19, no. 1 (March 1991): 1–14.

8. Ibid.

9. Shiraev and Sobel, *People and Their Opinions*, 307.

10. Gelb, *The Irony of Vietnam*, 24–26.

11. Thomas G. Paterson, ed., *Kennedy: Quest for Victory: American Foreign Policy, 1961–1963* (New York: Oxford University Press, 1989), 3, 123–24.

CHAPTER 5: 1968: NIXON DEFEATS HUMPHREY—LAW AND ORDER

1. Eugene McCarthy, National Security Archives Cold War Interviews, Episode 13: Make Love, Not War, 1999, http://www.gwu.edu/~nsarchiv/coldwar/interviews/episode-13/mccarthy1.html.

2. "Group Analysis of the 1968 Presidential Vote," *Congressional Quarterly Weekly Report* 26, no. 48 (November 1968): 3218.

3. Helmut Norpoth, "Primary Colors: A Mixed Blessing for Al Gore," *PS: Political Science & Politics* 34, no. 1 (March 2001): 45–48.

4. Richard Scammon and Ben Wattenberg, *The Real Majority* (New York: Primus, 1992), 5–19.

5. Adam Garfinkle, *Telltale Hearts: The Origins and the Impact of the Vietnam Antiwar Movement* (New York: St. Martin's Press, 1995), 7–33.

6. John Ehrlichman, interview for CNN Cold War Special Report, http://www.cnn.com/specials/cold.war.

7. Walter J. Stone and Ronald B. Rapoport, "It's Perot Stupid! The Legacy of the 1992 Perot Movement in the Major-Party System, 1994–2000," *PS: Political Science & Politics* 34, no. 1 (March 2001): 49–58.

8. Jack Valenti, National Security Archives Cold War Interviews, Episode 13: Make Love, Not War, 1999, http://www.gwu.edu/~nsarchiv/coldwar/interviews/episode-13/valenti1.html.

9. Charles Kaiser, *1968 in America: Music, Politics, Chaos, Counterculture, and the Shaping of a Generation* (New York: Grove Press, 1997), 5–6.

10. As reported by *Time*, October 25, 1968.

11. Shiraev and Sobel, *People and Their Opinions*, 237.

12. John Zaller, *The Nature and Origins of Mass Opinion* (New York: Cambridge University Press, 1996), 30–34.

13. Michael Balzano, "The Silent versus the New Majority," in *Richard Nixon: Politician, President, Administrator*, eds. Leon Friedman and William Levantrosser (New York: Greenwood Press, 1991), 259–75.

14. Richard Nixon, *Six Crises* (Garden City, NY: Doubleday, 1962).

CHAPTER 6: 2000: BUSH DEFEATS GORE—THE COURT DECIDES

1. Stone and Rapoport, "It's Perot Stupid!" 49–58.

2. Ed Gillespie, Speech at St. Anselm College Manchester, New Hampshire, December 3, 2003.

3. Shiraev and Sobel, *People and Their Opinions*, 122.

4. Christopher Wlezien, "On Forecasting the Presidential Vote," *PS: Political Science & Politics* 34, no. 1 (March 2001): 24–31.

5. Thomas Holbrook, "Forecasting with Mixed Economic Signals: A Cautionary Tale," *PS: Political Science & Politics* 34, no. 1 (March 2001): 39–44.

6. Richard L. Berke, "Many Seem Skeptical of Gore's Future," *New York Times*, December 17, 2000.

7. James E. Campbell, "The Referendum That Didn't Happen: The Forecasts of the 2000 Presidential Election," *PS: Political Science & Politics* 34, no. 1 (March 2001): 33–38.

8. Larry M. Bartels and John Zaller, "Presidential Vote Models: A Recount," *PS: Political Science & Politics* 34, no. 1 (March 2001): 8–20.

9. Henry E. Brady et al., "Law and Data: The Butterfly Ballot Episode," *PS: Political Science & Politics* 34, no. 1 (March 2001): 59–69.

10. Ibid.

11. Walter R. Mebane, "The Wrong Man Is President! Overvotes in the 2000 Presidential Election in Florida," *Perspectives on Politics* 2, no. 3 (September 2004): 525–35.
12. R. Morin, "The Exit Polls Face Extinction," *Washington Post*, March 16, 2000.
13. Wlezien, "On Forecasting the Presidential Vote," 24–31.
14. Bartels and Zaller, "Presidential Vote Models," 8–20.
15. Alan I. Abramowitz, "An Improved Model for Predicting Presidential Election Outcomes," *PS: Political Science & Politics* 21, no. 4 (December 1988): 843–47.
16. Albert Hunt, "The Gore Nightmare: We're Lucky Bush Is President—and It's the Republicans' Fault," *Wall Street Journal*, December 1, 2001.
17. Marianne Means, "If Gore Won, How Would He Be Doing?" *Seattle Post-Intelligencer*, October 25, 2001, http://seattlepi.nwsource.com/opinion/44036_means25.shtml.
18. Robert Parry, "The Training-Wheel President," *The Consortium*, May 20, 2002, http://www.consortiumnews.com/2002/052002a.html.
19. Jennifer Leblanc, "Al Gore," *IntheFray*, May 26, 2007, http://inthefray.org/content/view/2293/161.
20. Roger Simon, "Gore in Iraq," *Pajamas Media*, October 1, 2007, http://pajamasmedia.com/2007/10/gore_in_iraq.php.

CONCLUSION

1. Bartels and Zaller, "Presidential Vote Models," 8–20; Campbell, "The Referendum That Didn't Happen," 33–38; Abramowitz, "An Improved Model," 843–47; Stewart McCann, "Presidential Candidate Ages and the Cycles of American History," *Political Psychology* 16, no. 4 (1995): 749–55; Arthur Schlesinger, *The Cycles of American History* (Boston: Houghton Mifflin, 1986), 23–50; Wlezien, "On Forecasting the Presidential Vote," 24–31.
2. Shiraev and Sobel, *People and Their Opinions*, 197–99.
3. See Michael X. Delli Carpini and Scott Keeter, *What Americans Know about Politics and Why it Matters* (New Haven, CT: Yale University Press, 1996), 277–80.

BIBLIOGRAPHY

Abramowitz, Alan I. "An Improved Model for Predicting Presidential Election Outcomes." *PS: Political Science & Politics* 21, no. 4 (December 1988): 843–47.

Atkeson, Lonna Rae. "Divisive Primaries and General Election Outcomes: Another Look at Presidential Campaigns." *American Journal of Political Science* 42 (1998): 256–71.

Baker, Ray Stannard. *Woodrow Wilson, Life and Letters.* 8 vols. Garden City, NY: Doubleday, Page, 1927.

Balzano, Michael. "The Silent versus the New Majority." In *Richard Nixon: Politician, President, Administrator.* Edited by Leon Friedman and William Levantrosser. New York: Greenwood Press, 1991.

Barber, James D. *The Presidential Character: Predicting Performance in the White House.* Englewood Cliffs, NJ: Prentice Hall, 1985.

Bartels, Larry M., and John Zaller. "Presidential Vote Models: A Recount." *PS: Political Science & Politics* 34, no. 1 (March 2001): 8–20.

Berke, Richard L. "Many Seem Skeptical of Gore's Future." *New York Times,* December 17, 2000.

Brady, Henry E., Micheal C. Herron, Walter R. Mebane, Jr., Jasjeet Singh Sekhon, Kenneth W. Shotts, and Jonathan Band. "Law and Data: The Butterfly Ballot Episode." *PS: Political Science and Politics* 34, no. 1 (March 2001): 59–69.

Campbell, James E. "The Referendum That Didn't Happen: The Forecasts of the 2000 Presidential Election." *PS: Political Science & Politics* 34, no. 1 (March 2001): 33–38.

Carr, Edward. *What is History?* New York: St. Martin's Press, 1961.

Delli Carpini, Michael X., and Scott Keeter. *What Americans Know about Politics and Why It Matters.* New Haven, CT: Yale University Press, 1996.

Ferling, John. *Adams vs. Jefferson: The Tumultuous Election of 1800.* New York: Oxford University Press, 2004.

Fleming, D. F. "Woodrow Wilson and Collective Security Today." *Journal of Politics* 18, no. 4 (November 1956): 611–24.

Garfinkle, Adam. *Telltale Hearts: The Origins and the Impact of the Vietnam Antiwar Movement.* New York: St. Martin's Press, 1995.

Gelb, Leslie H. *The Irony of Vietnam: The System Worked.* With Richard K. Betts. Washington, DC: Brookings Institution, 1979.

George, Alexander, and Juliette George. *Woodrow Wilson and Colonel House: A Personality Study.* New York: J. Day, 1956.

Gillespie, Ed. Speech at St. Anselm College, Manchester, NH, December 3, 2003.

Greensteen, Fred. "The Impact of Personality on the End of the Cold War." *Political Psychology* 19, no. 1 (1998): 1–16.

"Group Analysis of the 1968 Presidential Vote." *Congressional Quarterly Weekly Report* 26, no. 48 (November 1968): 3218.

Friedman, L., and W. Levantrosser, eds. *Richard Nixon: Politician, President, Administrator.* New York: Greenwood Press, 1991.

Haworth, Paul Leland. *The Hayes-Tilden Disputed Presidential Election of 1876.* Cleveland: Burrows Brothers Company, 1906.

Hellmann, John, *The Kennedy Obsession: The American Myth of JFK.* New York: Columbia University Press, 1997.

Henretta, James. "Charles Evans Hughes and the Strange Death of Liberal America." *Law and History Review* 24, no. 1 (2006): http://www.historycooperative.org/journals/lhr/24.1/henretta.html.

Herring, Pendleton. "Woodrow Wilson, Then and Now." *PS: Political Science & Politics* 7, no. 3 (Summer 1974): 256–59.

Historical Statistics of the United States, Colonial Times to 1970. Washington, DC: U.S. Bureau of the Census, 2003.

Holbrook, Thomas. "Forecasting with Mixed Economic Signals: A Cautionary Tale." *PS: Political Science & Politics* 34, no. 1 (March 2001): 39–44.

Hunt, Albert. "The Gore Nightmare: We're Lucky Bush Is President— and It's the Republicans' Fault." *Wall Street Journal*, December 1, 2001.

Jacobs, Lawrence R., and Robert Y. Shapiro. "Issues, Candidate Image, and Priming: The Use of Private Polls in Kennedy's 1960 Presidential Campaign." *American Political Science Review* 88, no. 3 (September 1994): 527–40.

Kaiser, Charles. *1968 in America: Music, Politics, Chaos, Counterculture, and the Shaping of a Generation*. New York: Grove Press, 1997.

Kendrick, John. *Productivity Trends in the United States*. Princeton: Princeton University Press, 1961.

Kennedy, John F. *Why England Slept*. Garden City, NJ: Doubleday, 1962.

Larson, Edward J. *A Magnificent Catastrophe*. New York: Free Press, 2007.

Leblanc, Jennifer. "Al Gore." *IntheFray*, May 26, 2007. http://inthefray.org/content/view/2293/161.

Lippmann, Walter. *Men of Destiny*. New York: Macmillan, 1927.

Louria, Margot. "The Boldness of Charles Evan Hughes." *The National Interest*, June 22, 2003.

———. *Triumph and Downfall: America's Pursuit of Peace and Prosperity, 1921-1933*. Westport, CT: Greenwood Press, 2001.

McCann, Stewart. "Presidential Candidate Ages and the Cycles of American History." *Political Psychology* 16, no. 4 (1995): 749–55.

McCarthy, Eugene. National Security Archives Cold War Interviews. Episode 13: Make Love, Not War. 1999. http://www.gwu.edu/~nsarchiv/coldwar/interviews/episode-13/mccarthy1.html.

Means, Marianne. "If Gore Won, How Would He Be Doing?" *Seattle Post-Intelligencer*, October 25, 2001, http://seattlepi.nwsource.com/opinion/44036_means25.shtml.

Mebane, Walter R. "The Wrong Man Is President! Overvotes in the 2000 Presidential Election in Florida." *Perspectives on Politics* 2, no. 3 (September 2004): 525–35.

Morin, R. "The Exit Polls Face Extinction." *Washington Post*, March 16, 2000.

Morris, Roy, Jr. *Fraud of the Century: Rutherford B. Hayes, Samuel Tilden, and the Stolen Election of 1876*. New York: Simon & Schuster, 2003.

Narizny, K. "Both Guns and Butter, or Neither: Class Interests in the Political Economy of Rearmament." *American Political Science Review* 97, no. 2 (2003): 203–20.

Nelson, Anna K. "President Kennedy's National Security Policy: A Reconsideration." *Reviews in American History* 19, no. 1 (March 1991): 1–14.

Norpoth, Helmut. "Primary Colors: A Mixed Blessing for Al Gore." *PS: Political Science & Politics* 34, no. 1 (March 2001): 45–48.

Parry, Robert. "The Training-Wheel President," *The Consortium*, May 20, 2002, http://www.consortiumnews.com/2002/052002a.html.

Paterson, Thomas G., ed. *Kennedy: Quest for Victory: American Foreign Policy, 1961–1963*. New York: Oxford University Press, 1989.

Post, Jerrold M. "Woodrow Wilson Re-Examined: The Mind-Body Controversy Redux and Other Disputations." *Political Psychology* 4, no. 2 (June 1983): 289–306.

Prendergast, W. *The Catholic Voter in American Politics: The Passing of the Democratic Monolith*. Washington, DC: Georgetown University Press, 1999.

Pusey, Merlo J. *Charles Evans Hughes*. New York: Macmillan, 1951.

Rather, Dan, and Gary P. Gates. *The Palace Guard: Behind-the-Scenes Account of the Nixon Administration Prior to Watergate.* New York: Harper and Row, 1975.

Reeves, Richard. *President Kennedy: Profiles of Power.* New York: Simon & Schuster, 1994.

Schlesinger, Arthur. *A Thousand Days: John F. Kennedy in the White House.* Boston: Houghton Mifflin, 1965.

————. *The Cycles of American History.* Boston: Houghton Mifflin, 1986.

Simon, Roger, "Gore in Iraq." *Pajamas Media,* October 1, 2007, http://pajamasmedia.com/2007/10/gore_in_iraq.php.

Simonton, D. K. *Why Presidents Succeed: A Political Psychology of Leadership.* New Haven, CT: Yale University Press, 1987.

Stone, Walter J., and Ronald B. Rapoport. "It's Perot Stupid! The Legacy of the 1992 Perot Movement in the Major-Party System, 1994–2000." *PS: Political Science & Politics* 34, no. 1 (March 2001): 49–58.

Tetlock, Philip, Richard Lebow, and Geoffrey Perker, eds. *Unmaking the West: "What If" Scenarios That Rewrite History.* Ann Arbor: University of Michigan Press, 2006.

Turner, Henry. "Woodrow Wilson and Public Opinion." *Public Opinion Quarterly* 21, no. 4 (Winter 1957–58): 505–20.

Valenti, Jack. National Security Archives Cold War Interviews. Episode 13: Make Love, Not War. 1999. http://www.gwu.edu/~nsarchiv/coldwar/interviews/episode-13/valenti1.html.

Walker, Don D. "Woodrow Wilson and Walter Lippmann: A Narrative of Historical Imagery." *Western Political Quarterly* 12, no. 4 (December 1959): 939–47.

Scammon, Richard, and Ben Wattenberg. *The Real Majority*. New York: Primus, 1992.

White, Theodore. *The Making of the President*. New York: Atheneum, 1961.

Wimer, Kurt. "Woodrow Wilson's Plans to Enter the League of Nations through an Executive Agreement." *Western Political Quarterly* 11, no. 4 (December 1958): 800–12.

Wlezien, Christopher. "On Forecasting the Presidential Vote." *PS: Political Science & Politics* 34, no. 1 (March 2001): 24–31.

Zaller, John. *The Nature and Origins of Mass Opinion*. New York: Cambridge University Press, 1996.

INDEX

ABOUT THE AUTHORS

Robert Dudley is the chair of the Department of Public and International Affairs at George Mason University. He is the author or co-author of several books, including *American Government, 9th edition* (Houghton Mifflin, 2006), with Alan Gitelson and Melvin Dubnick; and *American Elections: The Rules Matter* (Longman, 2001), with Alan Gitelson. He lives in the Washington, D.C., area.

Eric Shiraev is a professor and senior research associate with George Mason's Center for Global Studies and research associate with the Institute for European, Russian, and Eurasian Studies of George Washington University. He is the author or co-author of several books, including *People and Their Opinions: Thinking Critically About Public Opinion* (Pearson, 2006), with Richard Sobel; and *America: Sovereign Defender or Cowboy Nation?* (Ashgate, 2005), with Vladimir Shlapentokh and Joshua Woods. He lives in the Washington, D.C., area.